$35.00

D0960866

Revolutionary War

AMERICA at WAR

Revolutionary War
UPDATED EDITION

BENTON MINKS AND LOUISE MINKS

JOHN S. BOWMAN
GENERAL EDITOR

Facts On File, Inc.

Revolutionary War, Updated Edition
Copyright © 2003, 1992 by Benton Minks and Louise Minks
Map pages 12, 25, 44, 51, 60, 66, 102, 111, 120, 125, 151, 156
copyright © 2003 by Facts On File
Map page 139 copyright © 2000 by Carl Waldman and Facts On File

Facts On File, Inc.
132 West 31st Street
New York NY 10001

Library of Congress Cataloging-in-Publication Data
Minks, Benton.
Revolutionary War / by Benton Minks and Louise Minks. — Updated ed.
p. cm. — (America at war)
Summary: A narrative account of the American Revolution, covering the origins of
disputes with Britain, profiles of the key figures, and descriptions of major battles.
Includes bibliographical references and index.
ISBN 0-8160-4936-X
1. United States—History—Revolution, 1775–1783[1. United States—History—
Revolution, 1775–1783.] I. Minks, Louise. II. Title. III. Series.
E208.M53 2003
973.3—dc21   2002007917

Facts On File books are available at special discounts when purchased in bulk quantities for businesses, associations, institutions, or sales promotions. Please call our
Special Sales Department in New York at (212) 967-8800 or (800) 322-8755.

You can find Facts On File on the World Wide Web at http://www.factsonfile.com

Text design by Erika K. Arroyo
Logo design by Smart Graphics
Maps by Dale Williams and Jeremy Eagle

Printed in the United States of America

MP FOF 10 9 8 7 6 5 4 3 2 1

This book is printed on acid-free paper.

Note on Photos

Many of the illustrations and photographs used in this book are old, historical images. The quality of the prints is not always up to modern standards, as in some cases the originals are from glass negatives or are damaged. The content of the illustrations, however, made their inclusion important despite problems in reproduction.

Contents

Preface

The American Revolution was a stunning event for its time and remains so today. Emerging nations around the globe still look to the Revolution as a model. They are impressed with its democratic ideals and the constitution that it inspired. Its many stories of individual sacrifice and dedication remain uncorrupted, even though new inquiries and interpretations continue to be written more than 225 years later. This book traces the building blocks leading toward revolution and the events of the war itself. It also explains how a young and disparate collection of colonies could take on the greatest empire and military power in the world and emerge victorious.

By 1776, only 13 years had passed since the Treaty of Paris in 1763. The treaty officially ended 100 years of hostilities between Great Britain and France. Terms of the treaty awarded Britain all of present-day Canada as well as all of the land east of the Mississippi River. Britain had conquered a territory many times the size of its island kingdom, but at a great price. The country's treasury was nearly bankrupt, and its soldiers were exhausted.

Once the French and Indian War ended in 1763, many of the British soldiers stayed behind to occupy the American colonies and help enforce English laws. Claiming the vast new North American territory was cause for British satisfaction and pride. The truth was, however, that the English were facing a problem they did not know how to manage. That problem was how to keep the American colonists under their control.

This account of the Revolution examines the impact of this newly acquired territory on the American colonies and their decision to go to war so soon after the French and Indian War. At first, Great Britain assumed it could expect the loyal allegiance of American farmers, merchants, tradespeople, and even politicians. After all, had not the homeland just completed a long and destructive campaign to protect them? The colonists should be grateful for the great victory England had won on their behalf.

King George III and the British Parliament miscalculated, however. True, the average working-class person in the American colonies recognized his or her historical and economic ties to Britain. These common folk and some of their leaders were not happy, though, with the prospects of being controlled by a government located across the ocean in Europe. The American colonists remembered that without their help, the British would not have succeeded in defeating the French. Men from Massachusetts, New York, Vermont, and Connecticut fought alongside the British. They had become seasoned warriors in their own right. The farmers and merchants of most of the northern colonies had helped provide food and other supplies for British troops and their officers. Many of those colonial citizens and their leaders felt they were perfectly capable of tending their own domestic affairs and did not need the opinions and direction of king or parliament.

This book shows how this spirit of colonial self-reliance was regarded by the British as impertinence, even arrogance. The British government had no tolerance for any sentiment in the colonies that did not conform to Britain's ambitions for the new territory it had conquered. Perhaps Britain's gravest mistake, though, was its decision to assume it had a right to control the great wealth emerging from North America. Britain maintained complete control of commerce between the colonies and other markets besides itself. It continued to reap the bulk of the benefits of this new world of astonishing resources and markets for its own goods. This volume explores the trade patterns between the American colonies and the rest of the world. It clarifies why it was in colonial interest to break from the British Empire and reap the rewards of such rich commerce themselves.

A primary British method to control growth and development in the colonies was taxation. The early frustration and rage the colonists felt toward England occurred because of attempts to regulate increasing prosperity. Ordinary, hardworking residents of the colonies were not far removed from their ancestors. They remembered that one of the principal motives for leaving England and risking a new livelihood in a hard and undeveloped new world was to escape the rigid control of English laws and regulations. Most despised were those rules that affected the

PREFACE

colonists' chances for improving their lives. It was unwise to threaten a shopkeeper trying to improve his family's future in Philadelphia or a yeoman farmer battling stony fields and poor climate in Connecticut. Such working-class folk in this colonial venture were willing to be patient to improve their prospects for a better life, but they had little patience with a government across the ocean that acted as though it were entitled to profit from their hard work.

With England's uncompromising determination to maintain economic and political control, resistance became more frequent and more public. As war became a possibility, many ordinary people became apprehensive. Not everyone, by any means, was happy about the prospect of separating from England. Even in rebellious Boston, before the British evacuated the city, it was risky for a colonist to openly side with the rebellion if he knew his neighbors opposed the war. Most colonial families were originally from Britain, and many of them still had family ties to the island nation.

When George Washington agreed to lead the Continental army, he was faced with enormous logistical problems, such as feeding and outfitting his troops. A larger threat to his plans was the low morale of men who left their homes and agreed to fight for almost nothing. Some feared the consequences of inflaming the world's strongest military power at the time. Many of the volunteers faced hostilities from their own families. For example, Benjamin Franklin was too old to fight himself, but he could not persuade his own son to support the Revolution.

Many conventional histories of the Revolutionary War tend to provide an oversimplified version that makes it seem as though all the colonists enthusiastically joined in a struggle for independence. In fact, as this account makes clear, throughout the colonies, especially in the early months of the war, many colonial families stayed loyal to the British Crown. These Loyalists saw themselves as English first and colonial Americans second. They were very skeptical that a new American government would be any improvement over rule by the Crown and Parliament. In addition to their feeling that open rebellion was a hopeless mistake, Loyalists were certain that the infant Continental army had little chance of success. Then there would be a terrible price to pay for anyone who had supported the Patriot cause. Some citizens tried to live between both sides, acting in a neutral manner but being extremely skeptical that the Americans could possibly win the war. True Loyalists openly supported the Crown, fought alongside British regulars and served as spies. If a Loyalist family could not stay within British lines for safety and comfort, it might flee to Canada or even back to Britain if necessary. In this volume, all these options for Loyalist activity are documented.

Between 1772 and 1774, tensions between the two sides became explosive. Helping to maintain and even increase these tensions were public figures who openly spoke out against British oppression. They encouraged ordinary citizens to use force in striking back. Some used every means available, including propaganda, to convince colonists they had little choice but total separation from England. Actions by activists such as Sam Adams were regarded as treason by the British. Had it not been for leaders such as Joseph Warren, John Adams, and Patrick Henry, public feelings might not have been aroused. Insight into the lives and contributions of these important figures and many others like them are included in this book.

In 1776, George Washington did not know what a difficult time lay ahead of him and his inexperienced army of Patriots. Washington was a successful landholder, a Virginia planter. He was not only wealthy, he was also an intelligent man who appreciated the role of music and other forms of culture in his life and society. The English and Europeans in general regarded the colonists as wild, rough-cut, peasant-class pioneers who had no sense of refinement or manners. George Washington, however, belonged to a social and intellectual class of colonials who had achieved almost aristocratic status. Several of the New England leaders of the Revolution were similarly from the intellectual and social elite. What is more remarkable, though, is that during the war itself, most all of these men, Washington included, were willing to endure many of the same hardships as the troops they led.

George Washington had proven he was a capable military commander when the English were battling the French in the French and Indian War. Yet he had no ambition to become a full-time army officer. When he was asked by colonial leaders to assemble an army to face the powerful British, he was somber and thoughtful. He reluctantly agreed but wrote home to his wife that he wished the honor had been offered to someone else. This book describes again and again why Washington was not only the right choice to command the ragged Continental troops but a brilliant choice.

There were many unsung heroes and heroines of the Revolutionary War. Some came from other countries, like Thaddeus Kościusko and

PREFACE

Casimir Pulaski of Poland, and some were simply common folk in the colonies who were crucial to the war's success. Often they are overlooked, and an effort has been made to include them in this book. Some were black, some Native American, many were poor and humble. While women did not play center-stage roles during the Revolutionary War, they aided in countless important ways. Many kept farms and small businesses going while husbands and sons served in the military. These women are also recognized in this account of the Revolutionary War. In European social structure, women had few rights and little power. But in Native American society, the role of women was quite different. This book highlights the powerful role of the Mohawk leader and negotiator Molly Brant, who is honored as one of the Founding Mothers of British Canada.

The name "Benedict Arnold" has been linked to the word *traitor* in most people's minds. The amazing story of Arnold's journey from ardent Patriot, naval commander, and military hero to despised traitor is an important one. It illustrates, again, how many people did not really believe that the war for independence could be won, or was worth so much sacrifice, and that piece of history is included in this book.

In many ways, the colonies were poorly prepared for a war of independence. They had no organized army or navy. There was no colonial manufacture of small arms, let alone cannon. Nothing was in place to keep a rebel fighting force fed or clothed. Perhaps the most serious disadvantage they faced, however, was that each colony regarded itself as a separate political body. Often, the colonies competed with each other in matters of trade and political influence. Southern colonies had a different agricultural and economic base than the colonies in the north. One task of this volume is to explain how 13 individual governments and social groups, often quite different from one another, united to fight for a new nation.

By the time the war started, slavery was already firmly a part of the economic and social system in Virginia, the Carolinas, Georgia, and Maryland. Much of the South's prosperity depended on the institution of slavery. When the war began, there were more than 500,000 slaves in the South. The part they would eventually play in the Revolution became a terrible dilemma for General Washington. In recent years, there has been growing interest and new research into the place of African Americans in colonial society and during the Revolution. Nearly every colonial regiment included black Americans. This book looks at the bargaining chip used by both sides of offering freedom to slaves who served as soldiers in war.

Others with no political voice but who greatly influenced events throughout the war were the American Indian nations. There was considerable difference in response among the Native peoples. Some struggled to maintain neutrality, some were strong supporters of the British, and some favored the colonial cause. In this book, for example, is a clearer picture of the self-destructive civil war within the huge Iroquois Confederacy as different factions chose different paths during the Revolution.

Who, then, responded to the first alarms in the New England villages outside Boston? Who was willing to risk business, home, and even life to take on a Goliath like Great Britain? This volume includes many personal stories of people of all ages and from numerous ethnic groups and classes of life who contributed to the war. When events unfolded in Lexington and Concord, simple shopkeepers and farmers emerged to gather on the commons and roadways in a standoff against the organized and well-equipped redcoats, as British troops were called. Fifteen-year-old boys who had never shot anything more threatening than a squirrel or deer stood shoulder to shoulder with their fathers and grandfathers, all waiting breathlessly as hundreds of seasoned British soldiers lined up and leveled their muskets less than 100 yards away. These colonial men were no army. They were just a band of neighbors who hoped they would not need to use their weapons. But someone, maybe just from nervousness, pulled a trigger, and the war began.

The popularity of the story of the American Revolution has never waned. Early diaries and accounts of Revolutionary War soldiers have been reprinted several times. Paul Revere wrote a number of accounts of his famous ride, and children still learn his story through Henry Wadsworth Longfellow's rhythmic poem, "The Midnight Ride of Paul Revere." Most people recognize pictures of the minuteman statue erected in 1837 at Concord Bridge. And many can repeat Ralph Waldo Emerson's famous lines engraved upon it, from his "Concord Hymn:"

> By the rude bridge that arched the flood,
> Their flag to April's breeze unfurled,
> Here once the embattled farmers stood
> And fired the shot heard 'round the world.

PREFACE

Years of careful study and examination of myths and memories surrounding the American Revolution have not tarnished the glow of that historic event. From the Freedom Trail in Boston to the national park at Yorktown, Virginia, most of the major sites of the American Revolution are visited each year by thousands of American citizens. The sites host extensive displays, walking tours, and educational films. "Living history" reenactors bring Revolutionary War events alive by acting them out as authentically as possible, frequently on the site of the event itself. As for books, new volumes appear each year, for all age groups, on some aspect of the Revolution. Broadway and Hollywood offer lively interpretations of the Revolution through musicals such as *1776* and the movie *The Patriot*, the latter based on southern colonial fighters during the Revolution. In *1776*, an important scene illustrates the powerful conflict between northern and southern colonies over slavery during the drafting of the Declaration of Independence. Jefferson's handwritten draft of the declaration rejected slavery. Southerners made it clear that if the antislavery clause remained in the declaration, they would not vote for independence. Without unity that included the southern colonies, the remainder of the 13 colonies knew they could not fight the British Empire and create a new nation. The antislavery clause was removed.

When Jefferson idealistically spoke out against British support of the slave system, he owned slaves himself. Without slave labor, Jefferson could never have maintained his elaborate property or rebuilt Monticello, his home, based on his original architectural design. New publications such as *Jefferson's Children, The Story of One American Family* (2000) explore the recent confirmation that Thomas Jefferson apparently had at least one child by his slave Sally Hemmings. This new material shows how difficult it can be to sort out the contradictions and inconsistencies in the lives of some major historical figures.

Important public television series such as *The American Revolution* and its extensive website, point out new understandings and reinforce solid research about the founding of the nation. In addition, other public broadcasting series, such as *Africans in America* (1998) and *500 Nations* (2001) introduce points of view from black American and Native American history that enrich the record of the Revolution.

As has been indicated at several points throughout this preface, this new edition makes its own contribution to a more nuanced and textured appreciation of the Revolutionary War. A major new feature is the inclusion of boxes interspersed within the chapters—short essays that explore in some detail all kinds of subjects that add a new dimension to the main narrative. New maps and new illustrations allow for more glimpses of events. A glossary defines many terms that may be unfamiliar. A significantly enlarged list of relevant books helps students and readers to pursue topics of special interest.

For most of the Revolutionary War, Gen. George Washington and his troops were outnumbered and outgunned. From the first shot at Lexington through the final siege at Yorktown, to the official end of the war in 1783, eight years passed. The Revolutionary War was second only to the nine-year Vietnam War in length. Even now, at the beginning of the 21st century, casual readers and scholarly historians are perplexed. How was it that so few people could muster the determination and sense of duty and idealism to suffer such a costly task for so long a time? The American Revolution was, by any standard of history, a wonder to behold, and this account both recounts that history and preserves its wonder.

1

HOLDING THE LINE ON BREED'S HILL, 1775

Throughout the night of June 16–17, 1775, a group of American colonists stumbled over boulders, tripped over one another, and slipped into ditches they were hastily digging. They worked frantically during the damp, dark hours as they piled up sod, granite, and stumps on top of a hill where the day before cattle had lazily grazed. The men had no time to lose. By dawn they needed to

Fortifying Breed's Hill in the night, June 16, 1775 *(Library of Congress)*

complete an earthen fortification in order to protect themselves against a feared enemy assault.

Using simple farm tools—picks, shovels, axes, and heavy pry bars for moving the biggest of the stones—this detachment of the New England army dug, slashed, cursed, and pried through the short night. Only the broken light from lanterns and the blaze from pine-knot torches kept them from battering each other.

The Charlestown Peninsula on which they worked was across the Charles River and not far from the colonial city of Boston. The only prominent features on its landscape were two hills. Named after the men who pastured their cattle there, the hill closest to Boston was Breed's Hill, and the other (the higher of the two), Bunker Hill. The Battle of Bunker Hill, though mistakenly named—it was actually fought on Breed's Hill—would forever be considered a turning point in the American colonists' fight for independence from England.

Quartered in Boston were hundreds of troops of His Majesty King George III. Some of them lived in tents, but many of the British regulars had moved into the homes of Boston families. Their commander, Thomas Gage, had orders from England to occupy the city and control the angry and rebellious colonials. General Gage's agents, or spies, had not prepared him for the savage fighting his troops would encounter from volunteers of the New England army on the morning of June 17.

The New England army was a different force from the one the British expected. There were not only Massachusetts militia—the famous "minutemen"—but also volunteers from Connecticut, Rhode Island, and New Hampshire. George Washington had been appointed general only one month before and was just beginning to gather together a united army from all the colonies—a Continental army. In Massachusetts, four officers were responsible for carrying out orders from Gen. Artemas Ward, headquartered in Cambridge on the present campus of Harvard University.

Senior General Ward and his advisers had decided that it was good strategy to secure Bunker Hill on the Charlestown Peninsula, but there was confusion among the men responsible for carrying out the plan. Gen. Israel Putnam was certain that Breed's Hill was the intended site, perhaps because it was closer to Boston.

Besides choosing the wrong hill to fortify, the New Englanders took the risk of digging in at the end of the peninsula, far from their only sources of food, water, and ammunition. Their supply lines could easily

HOLDING THE LINE ON BREED'S HILL, 1775

The Battle of Bunker Hill, June 17, 1775 *(Library of Congress)*

have been cut off by the British. With their muskets and six small cannons, they were no match for the many large British cannon placed along the Charles River shore and on ships in the river.

However, throughout that June night, the colonial volunteers continued to build their crude network of sod walls and trenches. They had dropped their farm tools, left their businesses, and ridden or walked great distances with determination to answer the call of the Committee of Safety. General Gage must not be allowed to set up his troops on the hills outside of Boston.

When General Gage discovered the work on Breed's Hill the morning of June 17, he responded by ordering his Boston troops in charge of cannon batteries to begin firing.

Common sense would have directed them to run off the peninsula, but the militiamen continued their work. Instead of choosing to cut off the New Englanders' supply lines, General Gage decided to attack the enemy head-on, an honorable but deadly tactic. To this task he appointed Sir William Howe, recently arrived from England to command the British troops in Boston. Howe's command was to ferry 2,300 British soldiers across the river and then march them up the slope of Breed's Hill, where half as many colonial volunteers waited nervously.

A contemporary engraving of the attack on Breed's Hill and the burning of Charlestown, June 17, 1775 *(National Archives, Still Pictures Branch, NWDNS-148-GW-448)*

In the heat of a mid-June sun, infantrymen in dazzling red and white uniforms began moving in ranks three deep toward the earthworks at the top of the hill. Each English soldier carried a heavy field pack with a ration of food, blankets, musket balls, and gunpowder. Colonial soldiers, on the other hand, had little water and food and only a few rounds of ammunition, with no easy way to get more.

No one can explain why the colonials did not panic and try to get off the peninsula while they still had time. For most of them, the glint of sunlight off the bayonets of hundreds of men moving up the hill threatened certain death. Stepping forward with machinelike precision, each English soldier had orders to climb over the walls the colonials had built if necessary and to attack with the bayonet.

The British did not break stride but continued as if they were a single unit. The only sounds were the rhythmic thud of thousands of boots pounding the sod, the rattling of drumheads, the shrill whistle of the fife, and the click of rifle butts rubbing against brass buckles.

"Don't fire until you see the whites of their eyes!" was the disciplined command from Col. William Prescott. When the British drew close enough at last, a single volley was aimed at them, without warning and

Dr. Joseph Warren
COMMITTED REVOLUTIONARY

DR. JOSEPH WARREN IS ONE OF THE LEAST-KNOWN leaders of the American Revolution, yet he was one of the most active and courageous. A native of Boston and a medical doctor, Warren attended the Stamp Act Congress and the First Continental Congress. He made a dramatic speech on the anniversary of the Boston Massacre in which he dressed in a Roman toga to address the gathered Bostonians. He urged them to arm themselves, withhold their taxes, and boycott all English goods. As chairman of the Massachusetts Committee of Safety, Warren was the chief strategist of the colony's early military planning, and he organized a network of spies to monitor British troop movements. "Should Europe empty all her force, we'll meet her in array," he proclaimed. His passionate words are considered some of the first steps toward independence.

After helping Paul Revere arrange for the signal lanterns in Old North Church, Warren barely escaped death at Lexington from a British musket ball. He then fought among the volunteers at the Battle of Bunker Hill (Breed's Hill) and was among the last to hold out against great odds. Warren was killed point blank at Breed's Hill. When General Gage later wrote these words to the British secretary of war, it was in part a tribute to Warren: "These people show a spirit and conduct against us they never showed against the French."

with surprising accuracy. Hundreds of Britain's proven soldiers went down, many of them never to fight again. Those who survived the first blast from the colonials ran, stumbled, and fell back to the base of the hill. They reformed their lines and marched forward again in the same steady rhythm. Once more the British forces met a colonial force that was waiting, and the musket fire was just as savage on the second round.

Unmercifully, the British officers commanded their men to attack a third time. Meanwhile, the colonials were almost out of musket shot. Some of them had only two more rounds at most, but many were helpless, with no ammunition and no bayonets. They were prepared to swing rifle butts and even to throw stones to defend themselves—but such a tactic was not necessary. The American officers wisely commanded an orderly retreat off the peninsula. When the British arrived at the barricades a third time, no one was waiting.

The cost to the British army was staggering: 1,504 men killed or wounded, more than half the 2,300 soldiers who began the fight. Colonial losses were estimated to be close to 500 dead or wounded. "Damn the rebels," reported a British officer, "that they would not flinch."

An even more serious loss to the English, however, was their loss of confidence in their superior strength. The most important benefit to the colonials was not so much their having proved themselves battleworthy, but the fact that they had done it as a united Continental army.

With the Battle of Breed's Hill, the forces of colonial resistance took the risky step of challenging the strongest military country in the world. Such a challenge was not rational and invited sure disaster. After Breed's Hill, there was little opportunity for the colonies to change direction and ask for forgiveness from Great Britain. The British had long regarded the French as their worst enemy, but in the spring of 1775 began a war among British subjects that would last almost seven years.

2
UNDERCURRENTS
OF RESISTANCE

Twenty-five years earlier, no American colonists would have been able to imagine the battle for Breed's Hill ever taking place. In 1750 some of the same colonial militiamen who fought on Breed's Hill were volunteering to serve side by side with the British regulars sent to America to protect them. There was a clear and common enemy: the French, threatening the English colonies from their strongholds in Canada. What happened by 1775 to bring events to such a dramatic turn? How did Englishmen living on different sides of the Atlantic Ocean cease to be comrades and become enemies?

From the founding of a trading post at Quebec in 1609 by Samuel Champlain, England's major rival in the race to settle the eastern half of North America was France. The territory that attracted both countries stretched from the Atlantic coast westward to the Mississippi River, and north from the Spanish settlements in Florida all the way to Hudson's Bay in Canada. It was an area much larger than France and England combined and was all wilderness, at least by European standards.

Once established, the small English colonies along the seacoast became essential to England as sources of natural materials like lumber and furs. They also provided markets for many goods manufactured in England. France, meanwhile, was concentrating on territory farther north, along the St. Lawrence River all the way to the Great Lakes. The French settlements were much smaller and farther apart and were usually little more than frontier trading posts. Only a few posts developed into city centers such as Montreal and Quebec.

Hoeing Different Rows
NEW ENGLAND YEOMAN
AND SOUTHERN PLANTER

BY THE TIME THE WAR STARTED, THE AMERICAN colonies boasted a dozen or so important cities and scores of towns. Boston, New York, and Philadelphia had become centers of commerce. Other cities such as Charleston, South Carolina; Savannah, Georgia; Baltimore, Maryland; and even Providence, Rhode Island, were not far behind in their rapid growth.

Early settlements in the American colonies sprang from a farmer's ambition to own and live off the bounty of his own land. Yankee farmers were called yeomen, and southern farmers were referred to as planters. Regardless of these different names, they all faced overwhelming tasks. They cut trees and pulled stumps to clear land, then dug ditches to drain soggy fields. New Englanders faced the additional task of removing stones from their fields every spring after winter frosts heaved new crops of rocks to the surface. Food and cash crops included oats, rye, wheat, maize (corn), rice, tobacco, and cotton; orchards and vineyards yielded many kinds of fruits.

\ Farmers' wives and children were an essential part of the labor force on any family farm. In addition to being a full-time cook and housekeeper, a farmwife was responsible for tending the poultry and other small animals, milking, and making butter and cheese⸗ She cultivated a kitchen garden of vegetables and herbs that would get the family through the winter. In both the North and the South, farmers became dependent on slave labor as well as their own. Before slavery became illegal in the North, slaves would help with logging, maple sugaring, butchering, and all the normal planting and harvesting chores. In the South, planters cultivated larger pieces of land to grow cash crops of indigo, rice, tobacco, and cotton. Their plantations needed a huge labor force to be successful, and when Indian slaves proved unsuccessful, they depended more and more on imported Africans, via the slave trade, for labor. There was no idle time for anyone on the family farm, but in both the North and the South, farmers became dependent on slave labor as well as their own.

The competition between England and France in North America increased during the 1600s. Most of the hostilities had started on the other side of the ocean, and from 1689 to 1763, in a series of wars, the

UNDERCURRENTS OF RESISTANCE

French and British fought each other viciously over control of territories in Europe and elsewhere in the world. It was not surprising, then, that at the same time the two imperial powers would also battle over control of the New World territories. In the French and Indian Wars, as they were called, the French and their Indian allies were pitted against the British and their Indian allies in North America.

With the signing of the Treaty of Paris between France and Britain in 1763, a new era began in the 13 American colonies. As a result of losing the war, France transferred a large portion of its enormous land holdings in the New World to the British. All of Canada then became British, and Britain's western border extended all the way to the Mississippi River. Spain's involvement in the wars also led to its loss of Florida to the English, completing the creation of a huge British colony that included all of eastern North America. This enormous increase in size put new pressures on the British in governing the coastal colonies.

Peace began in the 1760s with large numbers of British soldiers remaining in the colonies. The colonists themselves, however, felt less and less need for such protection. The colonies had "grown up" during the French and Indian Wars, becoming more resourceful and independent. As a result of having fought in these wars themselves, with their own colonial divisions, some of the colonists had learned new military skills. Some had even become officers. Ordinary people were now more confident and better prepared to carry on the responsibilities of their colonies, and their dreams of making better lives for themselves seemed to be much more within reach. In 1760 a Massachusetts man wrote:

> You cannot imagine what a land of health, plenty and contentment this
> is among all ranks, vastly improved within the last ten years. The war
> on this continent has been equally a blessing to the English subjects
> and a calamity to the French, especially in the Northern Colonies.

The land of "health, plenty and contentment" so glowingly described in 1760 was really a crazy-quilt collection of very different colonies. From the headlands of the Maine coast to the hot lowlands of Georgia, the American colonies were remarkably distinct from each other in countless ways. Even the two oldest—Virginia and Massachusetts—had different origins and social structures. Virginia had been founded by adventurous businessmen interested in maintaining their

An east view of the city of Philadelphia, 1768 *(National Archives, Still Pictures Branch, NWDNS-208-LU-25F-14)*

links with England. Massachusetts, on the other hand, was founded by Puritans intent on pursuing their own Protestant religion and village way of life away from the Church of England.

In addition to these two distant and distinct settlements, other colonies had attracted a diverse collection of people. In Maryland, many colonists were prosperous and highly educated, while in Georgia, settlers were the rejects of society rescued from debtor's prisons. Most of the colonists along the eastern seaboard spoke English, but some spoke Dutch, German, or Swedish. Almost one-third of the colonial population was composed of black people from Africa, imported as slaves and living primarily in the southern colonies. Regardless of their origins, whether idealistic, aristocratic, or profit-making, all the colonies by 1763 were governed by royal governors presiding over elected legislatures. Each colony had gone its own way for more than 150 years, and there was little reason to expect them to unite around any common cause.

A few large cities had developed along the coast, clustered around the most promising harbors. Boston, New York, Philadelphia, and Charleston were sophisticated and handsome, boasting fine homes and public buildings. By 1720, Boston had been compared favorably to London by an English traveler; Philadelphia was referred to as "a great and noble city" by Lord Adam Gordon in the 1760s. There was often a great difference in attitude and lifestyle, however, between the dwellers in

these cultured cities and others living more simply in each colony. The people who were farming hardscrabble plots miles inland from the coast often disagreed with the city folk. Even within the cities, dock laborers and servant-class families differed in many ways from merchants and the educated governing class.

With the end of the French and Indian War, the "crazy quilt" of colonies looked forward to peace and prosperity. But the British Empire had emerged from the long series of European and North American wars with a great debt. The very idea of establishing an empire was to create colonies to serve, support, and provide for the homeland. The empire should make it possible for the homeland to prosper and flourish. It was only natural, then, that Britain's response to its large war debt was to find ways for the American colonies to pay for the major share.

There were other points for potential friction. Great Britain was accustomed to controlling most activities in the colonies, so once the new French lands were added, it wanted strict control over them, too. The first decision was to keep all colonists out of the western territories transferred to the British by the French and to preserve them as Indian lands. That vast area included present-day West Virginia, Ohio, Kentucky, Tennessee, Indiana, Illinois, Michigan, Mississippi, and Alabama. By keeping the white settlers out of this region, the British hoped to

PRE-REVOLUTIONARY AMERICA, 1763

Ottawa
Quebec (BRITISH)
Passamaquoddy
Penobscot
Maine (Massachusetts Territory)
Abenaki
Lake Huron
Huron
Lake Ontario
New Hampshire
Boston
Mohawk
Oneida
Onondaga
Cayuga
Tuscarora
Seneca
Albany
Stockbridge
Mass.
Plymouth
New York
Lake Michigan
Lake Erie
Rhode Island
Connecticut
Pennsylvania
New York
Philadelphia
New Jersey
Miami
Maryland
Baltimore
Delaware
Indian Country
Virginia
Jamestown
Ohio R.
Shawnee
APPALACHIAN MOUNTAINS
ATLANTIC OCEAN
Cherokee
North Carolina
Mississippi R.
Chickasaw
Tennessee R.
South Carolina
Catawba
Charleston
N
Creek
Georgia
Disputed Territory
0   150 miles
0   150 km
Choctaw
West Florida (SPAIN)
East Florida (SPAIN)
Gulf of Mexico

Thirteen colonies, 1763
- - - - Colonial borders
━━━━ Proclamation Line of 1763
-·-·- Quebec boundary, 1763

avoid conflicts with the Indians. The colonists, however, saw the new
land as a wonderful opportunity for new homes, businesses, and trade.
When Great Britain issued the Proclamation of 1763 forbidding settlement in the new lands, the colonists simply ignored it.

Each year brought new attempts by Britain to have its American
colonies pay the empire's bills. George Grenville, chancellor of the
Exchequer in Britain (similar to the U.S. secretary of the treasury), had
the responsibility of paying off the empire's debt, and it was his idea

to gather in that money from the colonies. In 1764, the "Grenville acts" were passed by the Parliament in England to raise money in the colonies. They were the first laws ever passed by Great Britain to collect taxes to benefit only the Crown, with no benefit for the American colonies themselves.

The Revenue Act of 1764 (also known as the Sugar Act) increased some taxes already in place, such as on imported sugar and on goods shipped first to Britain and then on to the colonies. It added more taxes on cloth from other countries and on coffee and wine. Although these increases were annoying, Americans were even more angry at the attempt to enforce the earlier colonial trade laws and taxes established in the 1660s to earn money for Britain. The colonists had become excellent smugglers, avoiding taxes and control altogether. Strict enforcement of the trade laws by British seaport agents would cut into their profits immediately.

Another Grenville act, the Currency Act of 1764, stopped the printing of paper money in the colonies. Only English currency could be used. The southern colonies in particular had printed a great deal of their own money, and this money made it easier for people to pay their debts. Colonial paper money was not worth as much as English money, however, and Grenville knew that only English money could help to pay off English debts.

As soon as the Grenville acts were announced, protests began. In Boston, "no taxation without representation" became a favorite slogan. It expressed the colonists' anger that members of Parliament across the vast Atlantic could tax them at whim. The colonists could not elect representatives to go to Parliament in London to voice the concerns and interests of the colonies.

The British Parliament did not consider the debts already facing the colonies when it voted to increase their taxes. Most of the colonies had raised money of their own to equip their citizens to fight the French and the Indians. Now that the wars were over, they were struggling to pay their own debts. To be asked to pay the empire's debts as well simply inflamed the colonists' resentment.

On top of the additional taxes, the colonies were expected to pay all the expenses for housing and feeding the British troops through the Quartering Acts of 1765 and 1766. By this time, the remaining troops were resented and even feared, as these British soldiers became tools of enforcement for tax collectors. Colonies like New York, where most of

Stamps and the Revolution

AFTER THE FRENCH AND INDIAN WAR ENDED IN 1763, the British were deeply in debt for their costs to defeat the French. It seemed logical to tax the American colonies to repay those costs.

Among the new tax provisions was the Stamp Act, which Parliament approved in 1765. Stamp taxes had been required in England for many years. An actual stamp of approval was needed for some of the simplest procedures, and this way, England could profit from most daily business activities in the colonies. If a farmer purchased a new piece of equipment, for example, he had to have the official stamp visible on the receipt. These stamps had nothing to do with postage for sending mail. They were simply a convenient and inexpensive method for the British to tax the colonies.

The Stamp Act affected everyone, but merchants and city people felt its sting more than anyone else. They were the most likely to transfer property, arrange for liquor licenses, or make frequent legal transactions. They enjoyed more leisure activities using dice or playing cards, and buying them required stamps. Nearly every business sale, agreement, or service required a stamp. Enforcers of the Stamp Act could enter homes and businesses at will to challenge residents for proof that they had paid their stamp taxes; if arrested, the citizen was subject to a trial without a jury. Little wonder that the Stamp Act contributed so greatly to the colonists' movement to revolt.

the troops were placed, were furious. Supporting thousands of unwanted redcoats (as British soldiers were known) in local taverns and public buildings was bound to outrage the New Yorkers.

As if the Grenville acts of 1764 were not enough, the Stamp Act was imposed by Parliament on the frontier cousins in America, just to raise money to keep the troops in the colonies. Passed in 1765, this act required a colonist to prove a tax payment by going to a stamp office to have a stamp embossed on a document, or by using specially stamped paper. "Stamps" were required for newspapers and almanacs, ships' papers and insurance policies. Even dice and playing cards were taxed. Many different kinds of people were affected: tavern owners, lawyers, ship captains, printers, and merchants. Besides affecting a wide range of people, the Stamp Act came on top of all the other demands of the past two years. Economic hardship was already on the horizon for many, and this tax was seen as a cruel addition to the struggles of the colonists.

In May of 1765, with only six months to go before the stamps would be required, voices were raised loudly in protest up and down the seacoast from Maine to Virginia. The Stamp Act was another instance of "taxation without representation." In the House of Burgesses (the assembly elected by the colonists of Virginia), a forceful voice was raised by a brilliant speaker, Patrick Henry. Declaring the right of the colonies alone to tax themselves, Patrick Henry put into words the feelings of many people: "If this be treason, make the most of it!" While most of his fiery Virginia Resolutions were rejected by the House of Burgesses as too radical, they were printed and read all through the colonies. Beyond its economic impact, the Stamp Act was seen as a deliberate effort to weaken the colonies and make them more obedient.

In November 1765, just before the Stamp Act was to go into effect, James Otis of Massachusetts called upon all the colonies to send

The Stamp Act is denounced, 1765. *(Library of Congress)*

The Stamp Act is protested in the streets of New York, 1765. (The banner reads, England's Folly & America's Ruin.) *(Library of Congress)*

representatives to meet in New York. There the Stamp Act Congress gathered nine of the colonies in "an Assembly of the Greatest Ability I ever Yet saw," according to one of those attending. (Virginia, North Carolina, and Georgia were restrained from attending by their royal governors.) The congress was the first gathering of the colonists as Americans, not as New Yorkers or Connecticut men. The Declaration of Rights and Grievances voted by this assembly made Patrick Henry's cry an official declaration: Only the colonies had the right to place taxes on themselves.

While earnest and respectable leaders of the American colonies from north and south met at the Stamp Act Congress, defiance rumbled in the streets. A secret society in Boston named itself the "Sons of Liberty." Opposed to the Stamp Act, members of the society threatened stamp agents and looted and burned offices and homes. Upper-class citizens hid behind a secret identity along with the common folk; all took to the streets in various disguises, terrorizing those who did not oppose the Stamp Act outright. Eventually groups calling themselves "Sons of Liberty" emerged in every colony. Sometimes lubricated with wine and spirits, these unruly mobs managed in six months' time to force the resignation of all the colonial Stamp Act agents before the November 1, 1765, deadline when the act would begin.

In Boston, meanwhile, as early as 1764 the notion was emerging that all the colonies should unite to protest the increase and enforcement of taxes. To help promote this unity, the Massachusetts House of Representatives proposed to form a so-called Committee of Correspondence to maintain communication with similar committees, which it was hoped that other colonies would form. By 1773, other colonies were setting up similar committees.

Another unifying response of the colonies was the refusal to buy English goods until the Grenville acts were repealed. This boycott was planned to hurt the English merchants so much that they would demand that their government lift the regulations. The northern colonies in particular suffered from their decision to do without as many English goods as possible. Many jobs in the city harbors depended on the busy trade ships, most of them from English ports. As the boycott of English goods persisted, more than 900 merchants in the 13 colonies joined the effort to force the repeal of the Grenville acts and the Stamp Act. The British Parliament now found itself in quite a different kind of war from the one against the French and Indians.

If the colonies brought in neither profit from purchases nor taxes from government acts, Britain would suffer indeed. In Britain, alarmed merchants called for repeal as increasing numbers of them feared going out of business. Already in London as Pennsylvania's agent, Benjamin Franklin pleaded passionately in Parliament for the cause of all the colonies. He emphasized the debts already carried by the colonies

Benjamin Franklin (1706–90) *(Library of Congress)*

and warned that an attempt to enforce the Stamp Act would bring on rebellion.

By March 1766, one year after its passage, Parliament voted a full repeal of the Stamp Act. As news of this reached the colonies, Americans rang church bells, fired cannon, and held community feasts. Some Americans even took the occasion to express their loyalty and affection for England by celebrating King George III's birthday. Yet, successful as their efforts had been, one fact remained to haunt the colonies. Even though it had repealed the Stamp Act, Parliament upheld the right of England to tax the colonies, and the hated Revenue Act of 1764 remained in effect.

Now keenly aware of the American colonies' resentment of "internal" taxes—those on ways of conducting business—Britain decided to expand "external" taxes instead. The new Chancellor of the Exchequer, Charles Townshend, was not about to give up on having the colonies carry the debt burden. The Townshend Acts, increasing the taxes on imported goods such as tea, lead, paint, glass, and paper, were announced in 1767, only one year after the repeal of the Stamp Act.

The response in the American colonies was swift and predictable. Not only was this outrage unacceptable, it confirmed the colonists' fears. Britain would only continue to create new ways to drain resources from the American colonies and to enforce its will. Open search warrants, called Writs of Assistance, put colonial merchants at the mercy of the tax collectors. If an elected colonial assembly objected to the new taxes or to the writs, it would simply be dissolved. Up and down the coastline, beginning with Massachusetts in 1768, assembly after assembly was dissolved by its royal governor.

For the first time, Britain sent troops to America to enforce a tax, not to protect or assist the colonies. As redcoats filed off the ships in Boston and New York in 1768, the ugly temper left over from the Stamp Act days resurfaced. The Sons of Liberty had a new cause to rally around and new excuses for street marches and speeches.

Some of the colonists were more ready than others to step up their resistance to the acts of the British. Among the most outspoken were a group of Bostonians who regarded themselves as the true "Patriots." One night in September 1768, Samuel Adams, his cousin John Adams, Dr. Joseph Warren, Josiah Quincy, Jr., and Paul Revere met secretly at the home of Will Molineaux, a Boston merchant. Soon they found themselves discussing whether to hand out the town militia's muskets

Samuel Adams (1772–1803) *(Library of Congress, Prints & Photographs Division [LC-D416-256])*

to selected citizens in case there was a need to oppose British power. In the end, though, even the usually radical Sam Adams argued against doing so: Arming the people could bring unnecessary violence to the city, he claimed. Instead he urged a policy of "dignified non-cooperation." Lawyers John Adams and Josiah Quincy, Jr., urged the use of every legal means possible to remove the troops before considering force. Hesitating, Dr. Warren and Paul Revere, a silversmith and print engraver, finally agreed to abandon the idea of arming the city. There would have to be more creative ways to persuade the British to leave town and to alter the present course toward probable violence.

A boycott had worked against the Stamp Act. Why not try it one more time? Once again led by Massachusetts, most of the colonies joined forces in 1769 to reduce all purchases from England. Colonists encouraged local industry and began to substitute their own products for many favored English items. The impact on trade with England was dramatic, but so was the impact on other areas of life in the colonies. Tax collectors were attacked, and crowds demonstrated noisily outside the homes of merchants who continued to do business with England.

But the fact was that many colonists did not agree with either the policies or the activities promoted by the likes of Sam Adams. Although such "Patriots" were convinced that they were only trying to preserve rights the colonists had exercised until the French and Indian Wars ended in 1763, there were many others who saw no need to challenge the English. These people, known as Loyalists because they called for loyalty to King George III and the British Empire, tended to be from the more prosperous class of colonists. Indeed, many Americans of all classes and regions were coming to feel more threatened by some of their fellow colonists than by the laws or troops or taxes of the English.

Before long, however, the boycott was so successful that some members of Britain's Parliament were also calling for a change in policy. On March 5, 1770, Parliament repealed the offending Townshend Acts, with one exception: the tax on tea. This was a way of upholding the principle of Britain's right to tax the colonies. Little did the colonists realize, however, that another event on that very day in Boston would start a cycle of violent confrontation leading to the open warfare of Breed's Hill.

3

A MASSACRE AND
A TEA PARTY

By 1770, Bostonians were feeling irritable and tense as they went about their daily work. Their city had become increasingly crowded with British troops quartered in warehouses and public buildings, as Governor Thomas Hutchinson had asked England for more and more soldiers to enforce the Townshend Acts. Despised by the local people, the British soldiers were often caught up in arguments and fistfights with resentful residents. One civilian had already died as a result of just such a fight.

On the cold and damp evening of March 5, 1770, a group of Boston Harbor toughs began to throw snowballs at a lone British guard in front of the State House. They had no way of knowing that earlier that very day in London, the British Parliament had repealed most of the offensive Townshend Acts. A large crowd of men and boys began to join in, tormenting, shoving, yelling, and throwing stones. As the mob grew out of control, Capt. Thomas Preston called out a small unit of his guard to face the several hundred gathered. Somehow, in the desperation of the moment, a shot was fired by one of the cornered soldiers, followed by another. Caught in the surprise gunfire were 11 Bostonians, five of whom died either on the spot or later: Samuel Maverick, a young apprentice; an uninvolved bystander; and three combative sailors, including the large African-American man named Crispus Attucks, just off a whaling ship.

News of the "Boston Massacre" spread rapidly throughout the colonies, aided by a dramatic engraved image on a small poster, or broadside, drawn by Paul Revere. It exaggerated the facts by showing an

A MASSACRE AND A TEA PARTY

Paul Revere's engraving of the Boston Massacre, March 5, 1770
(*Library of Congress, Prints & Photographs Division [LC-USZ62-35522]*)

orderly squad of British soldiers firing in unison and with deliberation on a small band of innocent civilians, and claimed that seven, not five, colonists were killed. The immediate outrage in the colonies at this "bloody attack on peaceful citizens" passed rather quickly, however, as word of the March 5 repeal of the Townshend Acts in London brought cheers of relief to one seaport after another.

Samuel Adams, in many respects the most radical of the Patriots, was not willing to let people forget the Boston Massacre. For the next two years, he kept the memory of it alive through emotional yearly observances and even reenactments of the brutal event. But not all of the colonists were as extreme in their reactions. In fact, his own cousin, John Adams, and his friend, Josiah Quincy, Jr., actually defended Captain Preston and his men in court. The jury declared Preston and six of his men innocent, as having acted in self-defense, but two soldiers were found guilty of manslaughter. John Adams wrote in his diary: "Judgement of Death against these Soldiers would have been as foul a Stain upon this Country as the Executions of the Quakers or Witches, anciently. As the Evidence was, the Verdict of the Jury was exactly right."

➤ The various British efforts to impose taxes had repeatedly inflamed the colonists, but they were not yet ready to take the road to total rebellion. Prosperity swept through the American colonies after the March 1770 repeal of nearly all the Townshend Acts, and most colonists went about their business calmly for the next two years, relieved that no new taxes were issued from England. They hoped that nothing—and no one—would stir up more trouble. The tax on tea remained, but the London agent for Massachusetts, Pennsylvania, and Georgia, Benjamin Franklin, wrote from England, urging the colonists to remain quiet. Sam Adams, however, worried about his neighbors' willing silence. Finally, a series of irritations fed into Adams's waiting hands.

The new turn down the road to revolution was taken when the British Parliament once again passed an offensive act. Beginning in June of 1772, all colonial officials, including judges, would be paid by England, not by colonial assemblies. This simple announcement was clearly designed to bring the colonies more firmly under British control. Anyone being paid by the Crown and not by local citizens probably would enforce English laws more forcefully. This was all Sam Adams needed.

The Committees of Correspondence, first created in 1764 and mobilized during the Stamp Act, were quickly revived in Massachusetts under pressure from Sam Adams, and by February 1774 were established in every colony except North Carolina and Pennsylvania. Colonial suspicions were awakened again: What new limits and controls would be coming out of London? Notable citizens, including Patrick Henry and Thomas Jefferson, joined the Virginia Committee, while James Otis led the Boston Committee. The activities of the Committees of Correspondence rekindled the spirit of cooperation and unity that had developed during the Stamp Act crisis of 1765.

Loyalist supporters of England considered the committees so dangerous that they planted spies in some committees. The respected Dr. Benjamin Church of Boston sat in on all the critical meetings of the Patriots and even made stirring speeches in public criticizing British acts, but in November 1775 he was "utterly expelled" from the Massachusetts Provincial Congress as the first traitor to the Patriot cause. All along he had been sending secret information to the British about colonial plans.

A message of his finally fell into the wrong hands, and his identity as a spy was revealed, to the horror of Bostonians. Gen. George Washington presided over a military court that found Church guilty of "holding criminal correspondence with the enemy." Jailed for almost two years, Church sailed for the West Indies in 1778, but his ship was lost at sea.

The Committees of Correspondence were firmly in place just in time to respond to the next crisis, the Tea Act of 1773. Little did

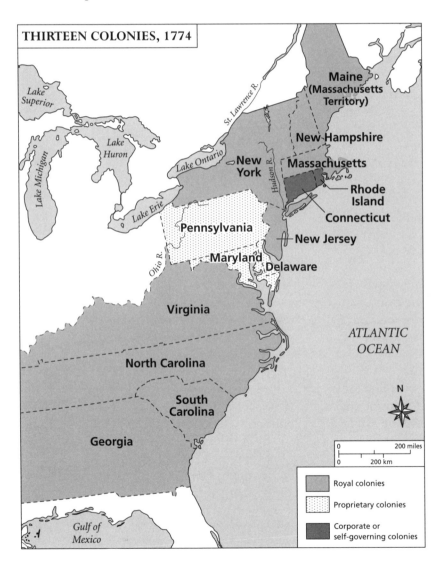

THIRTEEN COLONIES, 1774

Parliament suspect that this small remaining tax on such a luxury item would help to mobilize the 13 colonies to move toward independence— the same colonies that for more than 150 years had seemed unable or unwilling to unite for any common goal.

In 1773, the American colonists were still refusing to buy English tea because of the only remaining Townshend tax, and the East India Tea Company of London was facing financial ruin. The company's tea trade with India was considered very important to the British Empire, so Parliament knew it had to find a way to save the company from collapse. In May 1773, a clever solution to the problem gave the East India Tea Company complete control over the American trade market, with the right to sell its tea as cheaply as possible. Even the American smugglers could not sell their tea for less than the tea company could. Americans fumed at this tricky attempt to persuade colonists to buy the cheaper tea. It was time to show England again that they would not be bribed or fooled into abandoning their stand against unjust taxes.

As ships loaded with privileged East India tea began to land in seaports along the American coast, each colony reacted in scorn to this underhanded attempt to break colonial resistance. The Sons of Liberty took charge in the four ports expecting the tea, making special plans to prevent the tea from being sold—or even being unloaded at the docks.

Three East India Company ships arrived at Boston in December with their holds filled with tea chests to be unloaded. Governor Thomas Hutchinson was determined that these ships would dock and unload their cargo, and designated Loyalist merchants (such as his two sons) waited at harborside to market the new bargain tea and make a handy profit. As the first ship docked at Boston's Long Wharf, Sam Adams began to develop a plan of "dignified non-cooperation" that would send a clear message back to the East India Tea Co.: Business would not return to normal.

On the cold night of December 16, 1773, about 100 men disguised as Mohawk Indians and African Americans crept onto the ships' decks and hauled 342 tea chests from their holds. They acted in silence and secrecy, often not even knowing each other's identity. These Sons of Liberty threw the chests into the harbor, one by one, and then themselves disappeared into the darkness as the chests floated off on the tide.

By refusing to let the tea be unloaded at the wharf, Boston's Sons of Liberty made a bold statement to London merchants. This action was received so well in other cities that they responded in kind as other ships

The destruction of tea at Boston Harbor, December 16, 1773
(*Library of Congress*)

arrived. Tea was enthusiastically dumped into New York Harbor, while Charleston placed all its tea in storehouses, refusing to permit its sale. Years later, that stored tea turned into gold as it was auctioned off, one warehouse after another, to raise money for the colonial war effort against England.

While colonial response to the Boston Tea Party was one of delight at such a creative solution to the offending tea, reaction in England was strong, immediate, and nearly unanimous. In Parliament's eyes, such destruction of English property pushed the entire issue of colonial resistance to British taxes across an invisible line. It was now clearly colonial rebellion, and that could not be tolerated.

Almost everyone in Parliament was shocked at this radical behavior. There had always been arguments between certain members of Parliament and the leaders of the government about control of the American colonies. Deciding which taxes to place on the American colonies was cause for many an explosion, such as this one by Chancellor of the Exchequer Grenville after the Stamp Tax was repealed: "You are cowards, you are afraid of the Americans, you dare not tax America!" Townshend, as chancellor, did just that: He taxed America. Now the small, symbolic tea tax—the tax to prove England's right to tax the colonies—had produced an uproar and disgrace.

Angered at this insult to the empire, King George III began to take a personal interest in this turn of events in America. There had been far too much tolerance toward American complaints, he announced to his government, and the colonies had gotten out of control. The king began to take a personal interest in the "American problem," and he took it upon himself to instruct Lord North, Parliament's prime minister, as to the best action at each step. At the same time, others in Parliament resented the king's involvement, worrying about power shifting from the Parliament to the king.

It was King George III who decided that punishment was in order for the city of Boston. Against strong protests and speeches from friends of the colonies in Parliament such as the aging and ill William Pitt, the "Coercive Acts" were passed by the Parliament in March 1774. The king proudly announced, "The die is now cast. The Colonies must either submit or triumph." However, Edmund Burke warned Parliament that the Coercive Acts would only cause "a fierce spirit of liberty" to grow in America.

The Coercive Acts, intended to force, or coerce, the colonies into obedience, were indeed harsh and punitive. They were quickly declared the "Intolerable Acts" by angry colonists, serving effectively to unite the colonies in a new and forceful way against the British. To the horror of all the colonies, it was announced that on June 1, 1774, the port of Boston would be completely closed until the dumped tea was paid for. In May, British general Thomas Gage arrived to serve as colonial governor, replacing the royal governor, Thomas Hutchinson. More British troops also arrived, to be housed throughout the city—in private homes as well as inns and public buildings—under a new Quartering Act affecting all the colonies. Many Patriot families fled into the surrounding Suffolk County towns, and nervous Loyalists quickly packed up their goods to move into Boston. Closely watched and carefully guarded on June 1, Boston was effectively cut off from the outside world.

The Committees of Correspondence promptly spread the word up and down the Atlantic seaboard, and within days, support for the Bostonians came through in mail pouches carried by mounted messengers. Offers of harvest surplus, animals for slaughter, and ready cash came overland by way of Boston Neck, a strip of land connecting the city to the mainland. French and Indian War veteran Israel Putnam left Connecticut with flocks of sheep for Boston. New York pledged a 10-year supply of food, if need be, for the Massachusetts base of the Sons of Liberty.

A MASSACRE AND A TEA PARTY

King George III of England (1738–1820) *(Library of Congress)*

In an entirely different and certainly poorly timed move, the British government passed the Quebec Act in June 1774, shortly after the Intolerable Acts closed the port of Boston. In this act, designed to prevent the growing colonies from expanding illegally into Indian lands, the entire western territory north of the Ohio River became part of French-speaking Quebec. In addition, the Roman Catholic believers in Canada were granted full citizenship rights and freedom of religion, an action viewed as an insult and threat to the Protestant Christian majority in the 13

Thriving Colonial Trade Patterns

BY 1700, THE VOLUME OF FOREIGN TRADE OF THE English colonies was huge. Virginia and Maryland exported enormous amounts of tobacco to England, along with sugar and rice. Other raw materials such as indigo, animal skins, fish, furs, lumber, and grain were exchanged for dishware, glass, furniture, tools, and countless other manufactured goods that were not produced in the colonies. By the 1760s, the colonies provided 12 percent of all British imports and received 25 percent of its exports. English regulations forced all colonial goods to go through England first, where they were taxed before they went on to other countries.

Most profitable of all was the slave trade. A simple, efficient, and lucrative "triangle trade" occurred when New Englanders shipped rum to Africa and sold it for slaves. The slaves were delivered to Caribbean islands such as Jamaica, Barbados, and Guadeloupe, where they were sold for barrels of molasses. The molasses was shipped back to New England to be distilled into more rum. Not all colonies encouraged or supported the slave trade. Quaker Pennsylvania taxed it so heavily that "slavers," as slave ships were called, soon avoided Philadelphia altogether.

Boston was the busiest colonial seaport, and its fleet was huge. Only the English ports of London and Bristol were larger. By 1750, Massachusetts alone exported more than 2 million gallons of rum a year. The Revenue Act of 1764, also known as the "Sugar Act," with its tax on molasses, nearly ruined this prosperous trade. It was the closing of the port of Boston 10 years later, in 1774, that fueled revolution in many colonists. Without its vital seagoing trade, Boston's economy would die, fortunes would be lost, and the city would become desperate.

colonies. With these new developments, American colonists became convinced that the whole British approach to Canada and the western lands was to increase the stranglehold on the 13 colonies from a different angle, including giving special advantages to foreign French Catholics.

By the end of May 1774, a new note of urgency appeared in the messages distributed among the Committees of Correspondence. Since the announcement of the closing of the port of Boston, other Intolerable Acts had been announced, including the elimination of many elected offices in Massachusetts and of freely called town meetings. Leaders in distant colonies were shocked that many Massachusetts officials would now be appointed and dismissed by the king, and town meetings would assemble only with British approval.

If the citizens of Massachusetts could be punished so severely, who would be next? Was it possible that agreement with England could never be reached? People began to whisper "revolution" among themselves, some with hope, and some with fear, as they saw the road to war opening ahead of them. When the agitated Virginia House of Burgesses was dissolved by the royal governor, the burgesses simply regrouped in a nearby tavern to draft an official protest of the "hostile invasion" of Boston: "an attack made on one of our sister Colonies, to compel submission to arbitrary taxes, is an attack made on all British America." The burgesses then sent an urgent message to all the colonies to gather again, this time in Philadelphia, to resist tyranny.

On September 5, 1774, 55 colonial representatives from 12 colonies made their way to Philadelphia for the First Continental Congress. (Afraid of becoming involved in a larger conflict, the small Georgia colonial assembly defeated the attempt to name delegates to the congress.) Many of the men who gathered in Philadelphia had participated in the Stamp Act Congress back in 1765, and there was a sense of anticipation and seriousness at their meeting again, nine years later. The Virginians were determined to attend this time, and it was their elegant Peyton Randolph who was elected president. Philadelphians welcomed the assembly with generosity and style, also sensing the importance of the gathering.

It was agreed that each colony would have only one vote, no matter how many delegates were in attendance, and that all voting would remain secret. All through September and October of 1774, Carpenters Hall echoed with discussion and debate about the Coercive Acts and about devising an appropriate, united response. First, on September 17, the delegates approved the Suffolk Resolves from Massachusetts, drafted by Dr. Joseph Warren of Boston and delivered to Philadelphia by Paul Revere. A reaction by afflicted Boston and the rest of Suffolk County, its four resolutions urged that Massachusetts citizens arm themselves and operate a government separate from the British while Boston was cut off. Regarded by some as effectively "a declaration of war against Britain," the Resolves were nevertheless endorsed by the congress, setting the tone for the discussions that were to follow.

Men opposed to such radical declarations had come to the congress prepared to support a different way of governing the colonies of Great

Britain, a "plan of union." Joseph Galloway of Pennsylvania proposed two independent parliaments, a colonial body and one in Britain, with the king over all. Both bodies would have to agree in order for laws to be approved. The plan was discussed vigorously, but given the sentiment in favor of the Suffolk Resolves, support was lacking, and the plan was narrowly defeated on September 28.

Cautious delegates feared that all restraint would be abandoned, but by October 14, 1774, the thoughtful efforts of the First Continental Congress resulted in a series of strong statements and nonviolent actions rather than extreme recommendations. In a careful attempt to pull the colonies together in resistance to the Coercive Acts, the delegates simply denounced the acts themselves as unjust and cruel. A Declaration of Rights of colonial citizens was carefully drafted, which included the rights "to life, liberty and property" and to establish their own taxes. To back up the declaration, the congress created a Continental Association for strict enforcement of a total American boycott on buying, selling, and using English goods. While establishing a strong position, it fell far short of armed rebellion, which many feared might result from such emotional stands as the Suffolk Resolves. Yet there were clearly delegates beginning to speak of an "American revolution" to come.

The congress adjourned on October 22 after 51 days of deliberation. If the Coercive Acts still stood in May of 1775, the Continental Congress was prepared to meet again. The colonies waited impatiently as Parliament debated several plans in February 1775 to address American complaints but still preserve final authority in the hands of the British. Yet at the same time as genuine compromise measures were being considered, Parliament passed a Restraining Act on March 30, 1775, to control rebellious New Englanders. It would prevent the New England colonies from trading with anyone but Britain and its colonies and forbid fishing in some of the richest Atlantic waters off the New England coast.

While members of Parliament argued over the proper response to the actions of the First Continental Congress, John Hancock of Boston and Dr. Warren acted upon the Suffolk Resolves at home. They wasted no time in setting up a new colonial government separate from the British rule in Boston, and in alerting Massachusetts citizens to the possibility of war. When British troops marched north out of Boston and seized military supplies in Salem on February 26, 1775, the beginnings of war seemed at hand. A warning came directly from the mouth of Patrick Henry in Virginia's House of Burgesses one month later:

A MASSACRE AND A TEA PARTY

Patrick Henry
(1736–99)
(Library of Congress)

Our chains are forged. Their clanking may be heard on the plains of Boston! The war is inevitable—and let it come! I repeat it, sir, let it come! . . . The next gale that sweeps from the north will bring to our ears the clash of resounding arms! . . . Why stand we here idle? . . . I know not what course others may take; but as for me, give me liberty or give me death!

In the countryside outside Boston, towns such as Salem, Concord, and Lexington had been gathering military supplies, while on their town commons they were drilling their "minutemen"—men prepared to take up arms against the British "in a minute." There was an angry resolve to hold firm against British control as the winter of 1774–75 faded into springtime, and farmers outside Boston watched restlessly for another threatening move by British troops.

4

MINUTEMEN AND
MOUNTAIN BOYS

Springtime in colonial New England usually meant clearing new fields, plowing the stony ground and planting from sunup to sundown. In the spring of 1775, however, many Massachusetts farmers went to their fields at daybreak thinking about tensions increasing daily in and around Boston. For weeks there had been stories circulating throughout the Bay Colony that war with England was unavoidable. But any resistance by the minutemen who had been training all winter seemed inadequate in the face of the world's most powerful military forces.

The Second Continental Congress was preparing to meet again in May as planned, since the "intolerable" Coercive Acts were still very much in place. Every colony was also beginning to feel the pinch of the First Continental Congress's enforced bans on any purchase of British goods and any American trade with England.

Anti-British feelings were stronger in and around Boston in April 1775 than in any other colonial city. The New England capital had been choked for weeks by the intimidating presence of "lobsterbacks," a nickname for the redcoated British soldiers. Tension between Loyalists, thousands of British troops, and remaining Patriots in Boston added to a general feeling of approaching calamity within the city. British general Gage, responsible for maintaining control of Boston and the colony of Massachusetts, became uneasy when he sensed the restlessness of many of the colonists, and he feared a military uprising. Knowing the Second Continental Congress was gathering soon in Philadelphia, Gage

Boston's Old North Church *(Library of Congress, Prints & Photographs Division [LC-D4-11346])*

methodically continued his plans to seize or destroy any stockpiles of arms and ammunition he could find in the towns around Boston.

On Sunday, April 16, 1775, Paul Revere learned that General Gage was preparing to find and destroy Patriots' military supplies somewhere near Boston, possibly in Concord. The date of the actual march was unknown, but Revere began making plans immediately to alert Sam Adams and John Hancock in Lexington. Both men had left Boston days earlier to make sure they would get to Philadelphia for the Second Continental Congress.

Paul Revere
ARTIST AND PATRIOT

AS TALENTED ARTIST, CLEVER STRATEGIST, AND imaginative inventor, Paul Revere was an important leader in the American Revolution. By 1774, he was the official courier of the Provincial Congress, riding throughout the colonies with reports and correspondence. Revere is best known for his 1775 midnight ride to warn the citizens of Lexington and Concord that British troops were heading their way, but he continued to lead and to serve in many ways after that event.

His magnificent engraved silver punch bowl honored the Sons of Liberty. It was Revere's print shop engravings of the Boston Massacre that were distributed throughout the colonies. He designed the first official national seal and engraved the first Continental money in his shop. During the war, Revere learned a secret process of making gunpowder and helped establish munitions factories. In his foundry, he cast bells for churches and town halls, and he was the first in the colonies to roll copper into sheets to plate the Boston State House dome and sheath the USS *Constitution.* Although his one attempt at leading a military operation failed, Revere more than made up for this in his other contributions to the new nation.

Later that same day, Revere notified Colonel Conant in Charlestown that he would try to cross the Charles River and ride on to Lexington and Concord to spread the alarm if the British began to move in that direction. In case he was unable to get across, he would have someone send a signal using lanterns in the steeple of Old North Church in Boston—"one if by land, two if by sea," as the poet Longfellow wrote years later in his poem "Paul Revere's Ride." With this signal, watchmen on the other side of the river would know whether the redcoats were going to leave Boston overland by way of Boston Neck or by boat across the Charles River. Two days later, Revere learned that Concord was indeed the target. At dusk the British began dragging boats onto the bank of the river at the base of Boston Common. As planned, Revere instructed Robert Newman, young sexton of Old North Church, to light two lanterns.

About the same time Revere began his journey, William Dawes, a young shoemaker, left Boston to take the land route to Lexington as

The midnight ride of Paul Revere, April 18, 1775 *(Library of Congress)*

additional insurance that the message would get through. Revere himself wrote about crossing the river:

> I then went Home, took my Boots and Surtout [overcoat], and went to the North part of the Town, Where I had kept a Boat; two friends rowed me across Charles River. . . . They landed me on the Charlestown side.

Upon reaching Charlestown, he reported to Colonel Conant and began his historic ride on "a very good horse" he borrowed from Deacon John Larkin.

Soon after leaving Charlestown, Revere managed to escape a British patrol and ride on to Medford, where by his own account, "I awaked the Captain of the Minute men; and after that, I alarmed almost every House, till I got to Lexington." A short while later, Dawes arrived safely, joined by another volunteer rider, Dr. Samuel Prescott, and the three of them stopped at each house and awakened the occupants.

Paul Revere's ride had succeeded in denying the British the advantage of surprise. There were 38 minutemen standing self-consciously across the village common when the 700 redcoats came into Lexington. Their leader, Capt. John Parker, told them not to fire on the British but to break up and allow them to pass on through the village.

Before the minutemen could disperse, however, there was a single crack of a musket, and a skirmish began. It was over quickly, but the cost to the Patriots was enormous. Eight men had fallen dead, and another 10 were wounded; the British suffered only nine wounded.

News of the killing quickly reached Concord, where Col. James Barrett was organizing 250 minutemen from Concord and surrounding farms. While Barrett sent word to other nearby towns for help, Maj. John Buttrick led the 250 volunteers in a march toward Lexington. But when Buttrick heard the British coming to meet him, he took his men to the top of a low ridge that ran alongside the road and kept an eye on the redcoats as they filed into Concord. It was eight A.M., and the British stood at attention across the common at the Wright Tavern.

British lieutenant colonel Francis Smith set his men about completing the task they had been assigned. He was apprehensive about what had happened at Lexington, knowing he would have to give an account to General Gage. After searching every building, the redcoats finally

Concord Bridge—"The shot heard 'round the world" *(Library of Congress)*

found three cannon in the jail, and it was not long before they discovered musket shot stored along with barrels of flour at Ebenezer Hubbard's malthouse. The only building they damaged was the jail.

As his troops dismantled the cannon and heaved barrels of flour into the mill pond, Smith and his officers rested beneath a tree and enjoyed food and drink delivered from Wright's Tavern. The British then set fire to the gun carriages. When the fire threatened to spread to a nearby inn, the innkeeper complained, and one of the officers instructed the men to put out the flames. The gun carriages, which had been soaked in creosote, sent up clouds of black smoke.

While the search was going on in the village, seven companies of redcoats left town to find ammunition that was reportedly hidden at a farm two miles outside Concord. About 100 soldiers remained at Old North Bridge, while standing and watching nearby were 400 minutemen who had finally arrived from neighboring towns.

Neither side wanted to fight, but each soldier was prepared to fire if ordered. The minutemen, however, saw the black smoke coming from the bonfire on the common. When one of them shouted, "Will you let them burn the town down?" the volunteers gave a resounding, "NO!" and insisted they would at least put out the fire. They began marching, two abreast, back to the bridge. Commander Barrett then ordered his men to load their muskets but not to fire.

The British became increasingly anxious and began to retreat back across the bridge to Concord. Before they could all cross safely, however, there was an unexpected shot, probably from a frightened British soldier. Then the other redcoats turned and fired before running off the bridge. Major Buttrick, in the frenzy following the first volley, ordered, "Fire, for God's sake, fire!" The Patriots' first shots killed three British soldiers and wounded eight others. In a panic, the British turned and ran back to Concord. After much indecision, Colonel Smith ordered them to begin the march back to Boston.

There were no drums or fifes as the scarlet lines moved back toward Boston. Nothing happened on the quiet march until they reached Merriam's Corner, about a mile back toward Lexington. Waiting there behind any available cover were minutemen, many of them marksmen. Their accuracy was merciless, and one after another, redcoats collapsed along the dusty road. The British fired in return but could not see their targets, and all the way back to Lexington, the road was lined by stone walls concealing colonial snipers.

The Battle of Lexington, April 19, 1775 *(National Archives, Still Pictures Branch, NWDNS-JKH-JH-3)*

If General Gage had not sent relief forces under Hugh, earl of Percy to meet the returning troops, there would have been a complete massacre or surrender. Percy, however, arrived at Lexington in time to arrange his forces in a four-sided enclosure that provided safety for their exhausted brethren, who were by now running wildly to escape the minutemen. Percy also brought cannon with him, and it gave the Patriots pause when they saw one of the six-pound balls enter one side of a meetinghouse and pass out the other.

Under Lord Percy, the British troops began moving back toward Boston, followed and harassed all the way by minutemen. Before the redcoats were safely back in Charlestown at eight that evening, an estimated 3,500 colonials had responded to the call to arms. The British counted 73 killed, 174 wounded, and 26 missing. For the colonists, the numbers were 49 dead, 41 wounded, and five missing. Percy wrote in response to the fight, "Whoever looks upon them as an irregular mob, he'll find himself much mistaken."

The fighting at Lexington and Concord left little hope for a peaceful solution to differences between the disobedient colonies and the scolding, vengeful England. The flight of the British back to Boston was a major military victory in the eyes of the minutemen, and their morale soared. In reality, their action was an unplanned guerrilla tactic that had worked because the stronger enemy force had been caught by surprise. Many years later a famous son of Concord, Ralph Waldo Emerson, would preserve the memory of the event in his poem inscribed on the Minuteman statue at Concord Bridge.

News of the fighting on Lexington green moved swiftly south and west into Connecticut, Pennsylvania, New York, and New Jersey. Hard, steady riding through darkness and daylight spread the information to all 13 colonies. By May 7, 1775, less than three weeks from the day of "the shot heard 'round the world," the Committee of Safety in Charleston, South Carolina, received the message and began to muster troops to hurry to Massachusetts to join in fighting the redcoats. Soon, fighting men from Connecticut, Rhode Island, and New Hampshire began joining the minutemen in Massachusetts. Maryland, New Jersey, New York, and Pennsylvania sent volunteers soon after hearing the news. The closed port of Boston was soon surrounded by angry colonists.

Ironically, over in London Lord North had actually come up with a peace plan of sorts, the Conciliatory Propositions, and had managed to get them approved by Parliament. They were delivered to the colonies one day after the events in Lexington and Concord. Too little, too late, the propositions tried to soften the demand for taxes by accepting "voluntary contributions" instead. Hearing the report of the bloodshed at Lexington and Concord, many English people refused to believe North's assertion that he had never intended "to impose on our fellow subjects in America any terms inconsistent with the most perfect liberty." Britain's elder statesman William Pitt rejoiced at the news that the colonists had taken up arms to defend themselves.

By mid-May 1775, Harvard Yard in Cambridge had become a makeshift military camp. Thousands of volunteers arrived, most of them carrying their own muskets and at least a blanket. Some brought nothing but an eagerness to fight. Altogether, approximately 15,000 volunteers came to the camp hoping for a chance to whip the British. There was not enough food, water, or space to accommodate all the volunteers for more than a few days. Dr. Joseph Warren of Boston and old Artemas Ward of Shrewsbury arranged to keep the most skillful and experienced of these volunteers. They went about persuading the best candidates to sign up under oath to create an army of 8,000, about double the number of British soldiers in Boston.

While ordinary colonists were gathering in Cambridge, delegates from all the colonies were meeting in Philadelphia at the Second Continental Congress. Besides such issues as the closed port of Boston and the other "intolerable" acts of the British, those assembled knew that the real urgency now was a response to the attacks on their colonial countrymen at Lexington and Concord.

Even though they stood at war's gate, there were in fact still delegates who strongly opposed any further hostilities with England and favored more efforts toward peaceful settlement. The majority, however, voted to begin assembling an army from all the colonies, even though there was not yet a declaration of war. The military turn of events now required action and leadership, and the man most favored to command the armed forces was George Washington of Virginia, a veteran of the French and Indian Wars. Washington agreed to serve but did not take command of the Continental army in Cambridge until July 3, 1775, 10 weeks after Lexington and Concord. He had not yet arrived at his headquarters in Cambridge when the battle at Breed's Hill occurred.

Between April and June, the British under the direction of Adm. Samuel Graves worked to improve defenses by securing the hills around Boston, particularly Dorchester Heights to the south and Bunker Hill to the north in Charlestown. The gathered colonists waiting across the Charles River from Boston felt there was no turning back from the vicious British attacks on the two small Massachusetts villages in April. Now they would begin to plan specific military goals to prevent the redcoats from leaving Boston and becoming entrenched outside the city. Under the loose leadership of assorted militia officers, the colonists dug in on Breed's Hill, near Bunker Hill, and prepared to withstand an all-out attack by well-armed British troops. The dreaded assault came, but the colonists inflicted heavy casualties on the British at Breed's Hill in spite of confusion among both officers and militiamen. Colonial losses were serious, and the death of the beloved Dr. Joseph Warren of Boston by an enemy musketball was a great loss. There was no unified plan put together by a single officer and staff, but as a result of the battle, the American colonists gained new confidence in their ability to stand and fight the British, and British commander General Howe (who had replaced General Gage) knew he had to take his enemy seriously from now on.

After the June fight at Breed's Hill and throughout the remaining months of 1775, the British were unable to leave Boston except by sea. The colonials blocked all roads leading from the city and would not allow food and supplies from farms and shops outside the city to enter. British troops were not the only victims of the blockade. Hundreds of colonial Loyalists were also forced to submit to rationing of food and other necessities. More redcoats arrived from Britain, but the British still did not dare try to force their way through the land blockade. Meanwhile, the Second Continental Congress continued to meet, trying desperately to resolve the crisis. In spite of the appointment of Washington to command a "continental army," there were still lingering hopes that supporters of the colonies in England would persuade Parliament to accept a workable agreement so that both sides would stop short of war. Perhaps the colonial willingness to resort to weapons of war would convince the king that he must take their objections seriously. Before going home early in August, the congress worked steadily through the summer's heat and put two more plans in place: a postal service under Benjamin Franklin, and three commissioners of Indian affairs to negotiate peace treaties with the different tribes. When they resumed their work in mid-September 1775, they were joined by delegates from Georgia at last, making the congress finally representative of all 13 colonies. Still not officially at war, they took action as though they

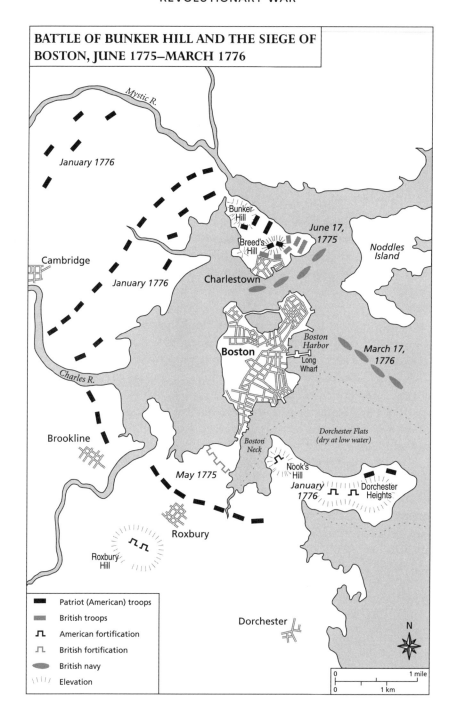

BATTLE OF BUNKER HILL AND THE SIEGE OF BOSTON, JUNE 1775–MARCH 1776

Mystic R.

January 1776

Bunker Hill

June 17, 1775

Breed's Hill

Noddles Island

Cambridge

January 1776

Charlestown

Boston Harbor

Boston

Long Wharf

March 17, 1776

Charles R.

Brookline

Dorchester Flats (dry at low water)

Boston Neck

May 1775

Nook's Hill

January 1776

Dorchester Heights

Roxbury

Roxbury Hill

Dorchester

Patriot (American) troops

British troops

American fortification

British fortification

British navy

Elevation

N

0   1 mile

0   1 km

MINUTEMEN AND MOUNTAIN BOYS

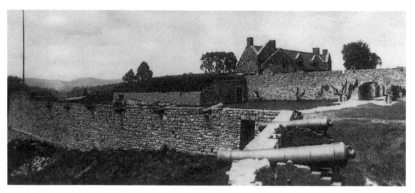

Fort Ticonderoga, New York *(National Archives)*

were. Col. John Glover of Marblehead, Massachusetts, began to convert six fishing boats into the first official, makeshift American navy.

All through the winter of 1775–76, the 13 colonies focused on Boston. Just as surely as the British could not break the colonial land blockade, the colonists could not force the hated redcoats from the city. The stalemate continued for months and would have gone on longer if Washington had not managed to find cannon to position on hills over-looking Boston. Using the heavy guns, the Patriots could shell the enemy and force them to leave the city.

The Continental army had begun the war under a tremendous dis-advantage compared with the British army when it came to artillery. At the very outset, the colonists had only what cannon, mortars, how-itzers, and artillery ammunition their militia had been able to take over from their former British masters. As the war proceeded, the colonists would capture some artillery pieces from British forts and ships; even-tually, too, the French began to supply some artillery. But the colonists had never even made any cannon until 1775, and to the end of the fighting, the British army would retain an advantage in artillery, espe-cially in experienced gunners.

Eventually the Continental army would assemble a fair number of mobile artillery pieces; most were made of bronze and ranged from three- to 24-pounders. (Some of the more stationary siege guns, the 18-, 24-, and 32-pounders, were made of iron.) The cannon were mostly muzzle-loaded but some were breech-loaded. The field pieces were pulled along by horses or oxen, usually with hired civilian drivers who led them to battlefields; there the military cannoneers maneuvered the

Forts Designed for Security

MOST OF THE FORTS THAT WERE CRUCIAL IN THE REVolutionary War were structures the British and French had built during the French and Indian War. The strategic vantage points that the forts protected in the early 1700s had not changed by the time the American Revolution began. Forts were usually built at vital places on rivers or the shores of lakes. Whole armies would move in boats down rivers or lakes as far as they could before going ashore and marching over rough paths through thick forests. Fort Ticonderoga, for example, stood guard on the narrow channel connecting Lake George with Lake Champlain, which then provided a route to Canada. Because of its vital location, Ticonderoga flew the flags of France, Britain, and the United States in the course of just a few years.

Many of the forts were simple wood structures consisting of crude buildings to house fewer than 100 troops and officers. Surrounding these interior barracks was a palisade of posts or planks set into the ground and extending eight or 10 feet above ground. Such structures did not hold up long under prolonged bombardment. The more durable forts, however, included stone walls and elaborate buildings, often taking years to construct. They accommodated hundreds of men in barracks, special quarters for officers, bake ovens, gunpowder storerooms, and everything needed for survival under siege. Small villages developed near the forts, with vegetable gardens, farm animals, and dwellings for the bakers, blacksmiths, and other support personnel.

The favored star shape for stone forts allowed occupants to defend the high walls (15 to 20 feet high) by delivering cross fire from the points. Deep trenches and earthworks added protection around the perimeter. Forts such as Niagara and Ticonderoga covered acres of ground. About the only way to destroy one of the great stone forts was to ignite the gunpowder or ammunition stored deep in the interior or in a bunker underground. A siege or surprise attack thus became the usual way of capturing one of these forts.

cannon with ropes. Each side of the wooden carriage had 21 rounds of ammunition to fire the various kinds of shot or projectiles—usually iron balls. The maximum effective range was about 1,200 yards; given the realities of untrained gunners and defective ammunition and weapons, the real range was more like 400 yards.

MINUTEMEN AND MOUNTAIN BOYS

"In the name of the Great Jehovah and the Continental Congress," Ethan Allen takes Fort Ticonderoga, May 10, 1775. *(National Archives, Still Pictures Branch, NWDNS-111-SC-94758)*

Although aware of the limitations of the colonials when it came to artillery, Washington knew that cannon could serve a vital role if he could bring some to bear on the British in Boston. The nearest location of such weapons, however, was more than 300 miles distant—Fort Ticonderoga in the Adirondack Mountains of New York. The old fort was in the hands of the colonists, thanks to a surprise raid that took place May 10, just three weeks after the conflicts at Lexington and Concord. Early that morning, two rival colonial officers awakened the British occupying Fort Ticonderoga at the southern end of Lake Champlain. The two commanders were Ethan Allen, with his Green Mountain Boys, and Benedict Arnold. Neither had known of the other's plans when he set about to attack the fort, for each was acting under different but similar orders from two separate colonies—Connecticut and Massachusetts. The two colonies had recognized the strategic location of the fort commanding the great Lake Champlain and the valley passage south from Canada. Once shots were fired at Lexington and Concord and war seemed painfully near, both colonies rushed to secure that critical back-door entrance from Canada that the British would surely use.

Lieutenant Feltham, the fort's commander, had no time to fully dress when he stood at the door of his quarters early that May morning and heard Ethan Allen demand (according to Allen's later claim), "In the name of the Great Jehovah and the Continental Congress, come out, you old rat!" Feltham surrendered, and the old fort fell to the American colonists without a shot. The fort was a virtual treasury of artillery—some 78 serviceable cannon (mostly four-, six- and 12-pounders), six mortars, three howitzers, and thousands of cannonballs—but the weapons were of little value to the Patriots as long as they remained at this remote fort. Transporting such cargo any distance would test the ingenuity of even the best engineer.

When George Washington took command of the Continental army on July 3, 1775, his first goal was to drive the British from Boston. After he decided that this called for artillery, late that fall he sent Henry Knox, formerly a Boston bookseller, to Ticonderoga to begin the operation of

Teams of oxen are used to haul guns from Fort Ticonderoga to the siege of Boston, December 1775–January 1776. *(National Archives)*

moving some of the cannon captured there. Knox arrived at the old, crumbling fortress on December 5, 1775, and announced his intentions. The men occupying the quarters stood in disbelief. The task of moving heavy artillery across rough terrain in winter conditions seemed impossible. Knox, however, would not be discouraged. Although he had no military experience, he was full of enthusiasm for the Patriots' cause. He selected about 60 cannon and mortars, as well as most of the available ammunition, and then, in mid-December, set off for Boston. Using some 42 sledges and 80 yoke of oxen, and occasionally resorting to barges, Knox led his men for about five weeks through the cold and snow, arriving in Cambridge on January 24, 1776, with the artillery.

Soon Washington had the cannon placed on the heights surrounding Boston. The British tried once to attack the gun emplacements but they were driven back by a severe storm. Finally giving in to the colonial guns looming over his troops, Gen. William Howe formed a flotilla of ships on March 17, 1776, to carry all the redcoats in Boston—and many Loyalists who chose to leave—up the coast to Halifax in Nova Scotia, Canada. The eight-month occupation of Boston had ended. The very next day, a Sunday, Washington entered the city and attended a worship service in thanksgiving.

5

THE FIRST CAMPAIGNS

When George Washington assumed command of the Continental army in July 1775, he faced what might have seemed to many as insurmountable disadvantages in comparison with the British forces he was about to confront. To begin with, there would soon be shortages of food and clothing for the American troops—shortages that would persist in most places throughout most of the war. The American colonists had long relied heavily on England for manufactured goods and other supplies. Thus, the very acts of the 1774 Continental Association that had cut off trade with Britain and its other colonies actually hurt the American colonies severely, and the British navy would make it difficult to obtain imports throughout the war. Many American troops, for instance, did not have proper uniforms; more important, they were often short of proper footwear for the long marches and of blankets for the cold nights. Food supplies were sometimes so scarce that soldiers were reduced to desperate near-starvation diets.

Gunpowder and ammunition would also remain in extremely short supply throughout the years of the war, and weapons themselves were hard to come by. In fact, in the early months of the war most of the American soldiers had to supply their own weapons. Those who had served as officers under the British or in local militia tended to own swords as symbols of status. Cavalry troops acquired sabers. Both of these groups also tended to favor pistols—the primitive flintlock type, and not really of much use in the heat of battle.

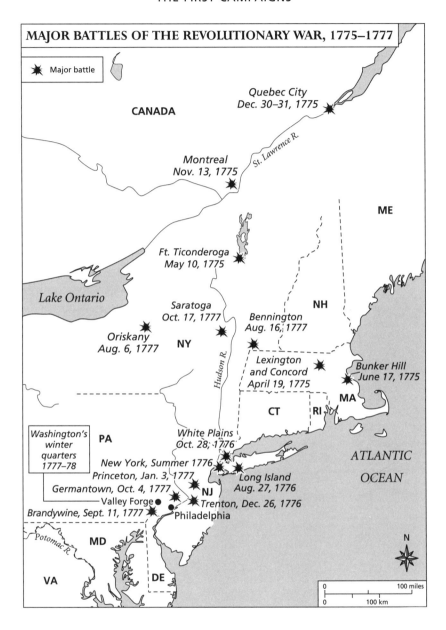

MAJOR BATTLES OF THE REVOLUTIONARY WAR, 1775–1777

✴ Major battle

CANADA

Quebec City
Dec. 30–31, 1775

St. Lawrence R.

Montreal
Nov. 13, 1775

ME

Ft. Ticonderoga
May 10, 1775

Lake Ontario

Saratoga
Oct. 17, 1777

NH

Bennington
Aug. 16, 1777

Oriskany
Aug. 6, 1777

NY

Hudson R.

Lexington
and Concord
April 19, 1775

Bunker Hill
June 17, 1775

MA

CT RI

Washington's
winter
quarters
1777–78

PA

White Plains
Oct. 28, 1776

New York, Summer 1776
Princeton, Jan. 3, 1777
Germantown, Oct. 4, 1777
Valley Forge
Brandywine, Sept. 11, 1777

NJ

Long Island
Aug. 27, 1776

Trenton, Dec. 26, 1776
Philadelphia

ATLANTIC
OCEAN

Potomac R.

MD

VA

DE

N

0   100 miles
0   100 km

But the basic weapon for the mass of American soldiers was the
musket. The barrels of these muskets, extending from 36 to 46 inches in
length, were smoothbore and usually took about a .75 caliber bullet

Revolutionary War musket *(Catalog of Francis Bannerman Sons, New York, N.Y.)*

(that is, one with a $3/4$-inch diameter). Muskets also had a bayonet that could be attached to the front of the barrel. A musket was muzzle-loaded, meaning a cartridge of gunpowder and a lead ball wrapped in paper or cloth were jammed down into the barrel with a ramrod; the spark was provided by a flintlock—a piece of flint that, when released by the spring lock, struck against a piece of steel to cause a spark that ignited the powder in the "touch hole." This flint had to be replaced fairly frequently. Even with a sharp flint and a clean "touch hole," a flintlock fired only about 70 percent of the time; dampness was a major problem—"keep your powder dry" was a literal admonition. And even when all went well, such a musket was apt to be accurate only up to about 100 yards.

Most of the colonial troops showed up at the outset of the war with their own locally made muskets. Very quickly, though, the Committees of Safety, which effectively took over the operations of each of the colonies, were contracting with gunsmiths to make a fairly standardized musket—not that different, in fact, from the basic musket used by the British. When the French got into the war, they sent over large quantities of French army muskets.

Then there were the famous long-barreled American rifles—often known as the Kentucky rifle, but actually originating in Pennsylvania with immigrant German gunsmiths. Also muzzle-loaded and with a flintlock, the rifle was primarily distinguished from a musket by the fact that its barrel was grooved, or "rifled"; this gave a spin to the ball as it moved through the barrel and so increased its speed, force, and accuracy: a skilled rifleman could be accurate up to 300 yards. On the other hand, a rifle had to be loaded with greater precision and thus took longer to load and to be fired. Thus, rifles tended to be used by special units of sharpshooters, assigned to pick off individual men. Rifles, in addition, did not traditionally have a bayonet, so they were of no use in close combat.

But accuracy in firing an individual weapon was not especially required from muskets. For the most part, the standard method of fighting a battle in those days was to line up the troops defending a position and then, with an officer or noncommissioned officer shouting the commands to load and fire, have them shoot off volleys. Well-drilled soldiers could load and fire about four times a minute; since the fire was accurate up to 100 yards, and the last 100 yards might take the attacking troops that minute to cross, the attackers would be exposed to perhaps four volleys, the traditional "wall of fire." There was little need to aim at an individual soldier.

British troops also carried muskets, the standard model being the "Brown Bess." (The origins of that name are somewhat uncertain, but it is now believed that the "Bess" is a play on the word "buss" in "blunder-buss"—in turn, a corruption of the German for "thunder-box"—while brown refers to the color of the wooden stock and/or barrel.) But not only were the British better equipped and armed in the early years of the war; they were also far more skilled in the tactics of the day. Both the British regulars and the German mercenaries had been drilled and drilled, and they knew well how to stand and fire volleys from formations. They also knew how to charge with fixed bayonets—often the only way to conclude an engagement; such close fighting with bayonets required both bravery and skill. The colonists may have had plenty of the former but little practice in bayonet combat. And except for a few of the more elite units, most American troops had little experience in the tight formations and rigid commands employed in firing volleys. The American forces, in fact, often lacked a clear hierarchy of command, with officers often disagreeing as to who was in charge at particular battles. None of this helped the morale of the colonial troops.

Of course, everyone—British and American—expected the war to be over in a year or so. Only a few, like John Adams, warned of a "long, obstinate and bloody war." Those who had fought at Breed's Hill, for instance, were planning to return home in a few months, and the turnover of American soldiers who enlisted for six or eight months remained a severe problem throughout most of the war. No sooner were they adequately trained and experienced in the field than some soldiers' terms of duty were over. Such a system of enlistments was aggravated by the fact that pay was often late in coming; when soldiers heard from their families at home that they were in desperate straits—or that the harvest needed to be brought in—the soldiers often simply

George Washington surrounded by a Native American warrior and uniformed Hessian, British, and French soldiers *(Library of Congress, Prints & Photographs Division [LC-USZ62-47827])*

deserted. No wonder that throughout the war various colonial units would rise up in mutiny.

But all was not to the disadvantage of the American colonial troops. Especially in the early years of the war, they were eager to serve, loyal to their officers, and determined to fight against overwhelming odds. This was a great advantage to General Washington. These soldiers were also fighting on their home ground, in a huge land that was very different from England. One volunteer expressed it well when he said, "In the Woods, we shall be a Match for them, and was their number trebled have I the least doubt, but we should be superior to them in force as we are in Virtue."

The British regular soldiers, or "lobsterbacks," on the other hand, came well equipped and well trained but unmotivated. While proud of their reputation as being part of the most powerful army in the world, they were not convinced that the colonial uprising was worth their best efforts. This proved to be a major advantage for the colonials. Added to that, the arrogance of British officers was well known, and many of them were simply wealthy men's sons who had bought their officer's commissions.

The British even found it necessary to hire foreign soldiers to fill the ranks serving in the colonies, since the American conflict was not a popular cause for recruitment at home. The high desertion rate of British troops in America, even as early as 1774 when Boston Harbor was closed, indicated the lack of loyalty to the king's cause. In desperation, the British turned to various German princes to provide trained soldiers to fight British battles in America—for a large fee, of course. Many of the soldiers were sent by the prince of Hesse, so all the German soldiers became known as "Hessians" to the Americans. Like the British regulars, these professional soldiers from Germany were well trained, well equipped, and well disciplined. Many were young men forced into the army against their will, however, and they served under cruel rules and harsh officers. In fact, the Americans often discovered the German soldiers to be sympathetic to their rebellion, surrendering instead of fighting. Hessians deserted at such a high rate in America that by the end of the war, only about half as many returned as had landed on American shores.

The Continental army faced the added disadvantage of having few trained and experienced officers. A few military leaders, such as Israel Putnam, remained from the French and Indian Wars, but General

REVOLUTIONARY WAR

Marquis de Lafayette
(1737–1834)
(National Archives)

Washington needed many more. He was grateful to receive offers of help from European officers attracted to the colonial pursuit of liberty against the mighty British Empire. Only 20 years old, officer Thaddeus Kościusko left the Polish army in 1776 to serve under Washington. He supervised the construction of forts along the Delaware River as well as the early development of the great fort at West Point on the Hudson River. Count Casimir Pulaski, also from Poland, led the colonial cavalry until his death at the head of his troops in 1780. Others from Europe were Johann Kalb of Bavaria (who called himself "Baron de Kalb") and Baron von Steuben of Prussia. It was to von Steuben that Washington entrusted the training of his troops. His organization and experience were critical in transforming the green, or inexperienced, colonial recruits into effective soldiers.

It was the marquis de Lafayette, however, who truly captured the hearts of the colonials, soldiers and civilians alike. Only 20 years old when he began his command under Washington in July 1777, he believed passionately in the American cause. He used his own fortune to equip and feed the rebel troops under his command. A hero on the battlefield, Lafayette's intelligence and graciousness also made him a favorite guest in the parlor.

Problems with ill-prepared soldiers and inadequate supplies kept the colonists at a disadvantage throughout the first third of the American Revolution. There were two early campaigns, in particular, that illustrated the clumsiness and hardship of the Continental army. The first was the 1775–76 attempt to capture Quebec and seize all of Canada, before independence had been declared; the second happened eight months later in 1776, when General Washington's plan to hold on to New York City failed.

The plan to invade Canada began to take shape with the seizure of Fort Ticonderoga in May 1775, just three weeks after the fighting at Lexington and Concord. The surprise assault on the old British fortress was a mistake, according to some delegates at the Second Continental Congress. It would give Parliament and the king just one more reason to punish the colonies. These representatives favored some kind of a compromise with their countrymen.

Other voices in the congress, however, saw the taking of Ticonderoga as an unexpected opportunity. The old fort on Lake Champlain could become a staging point for a thrust into British-owned Canada. Control of Canada would eliminate the threat of an enemy attack from the north. Even more attractive, though, was the possibility that Canada (all of eastern North America north of the St. Lawrence River) would become a 14th American colony. The great landmass would more than double the area of the thirteen colonies.

Hoping that the Canadians might welcome an opportunity to support colonial resistance to the English, the Continental Congress sent a message to Gen. Philip Schuyler, one of Washington's four major generals and the commander at Fort Ticonderoga. The message made a vague suggestion that Schuyler should move to capture Fort St. Johns just north of Lake Champlain, Montreal, and any other parts of Canada "if he finds it practical . . . and not disagreeable to the Canadians." Schuyler received the message at a time when conditions at Fort Ticonderoga were in a shambles. Soldiers there were indifferent to discipline and order. They did not bother to keep themselves or their quarters clean, and their carelessness

Two Colonial Cities
BOSTON AND QUEBEC

WITH ITS EXCELLENT HARBOR, BOSTON IN 1776 WAS A busy, thoroughly English town. It was the third largest city in the colonies, after Philadelphia and New York. Like a balloon on a string, the hilly Shawmut peninsula was connected to the mainland by slender "Boston Neck." Boston's 17,000 residents were industrious merchants and small farmers, seafarers and fine craftspeople. Most workers lived in cramped neighborhoods, but many Boston homes were accented with fine gardens. Almost every activity and every product made in Boston related to the sea.

Boston's wharves thrust out from every inch of shore. The Long Wharf was the largest and most developed, leading directly to the State House and markets, the heart of the city. Scattered around the peninsula were "ropewalk" factories that made ships' rigging and chandlers that provided ships' supplies. Warehouses, distilleries, and small shops lined the shore. Boston's flourishing trade sent its ships around the world. Boston was also a religious city; at the time of the Revolution it was a strongly Protestant city. By 1776 it had Baptists, Quakers, French Protestants, Presbyterians, Anglicans (Episcopalians), and countless Congregationalists.

On the other hand, Quebec, located on a massive outcrop of rock overlooking the St. Lawrence River, was still a thoroughly French and Roman Catholic city. In 1776, it had been in British hands for only 13 years. The Roman Catholic spires, elegant homes, and government buildings marked the skyline of the Upper City, center of French religion, government, and culture during its decades as capital of New France.

The poorer and working classes lived in the Lower Town along the river, where steep, twisting, and narrow streets connected their homes, small shops, and docks to the Upper Town. Since the unsuitable climate and soil around the city made farming unprofitable, French settlers who lived outside the city struggled to stay alive. Quebec had been dependent on France for most of its food and supplies, and this dependency was what maintained the city's "Frenchness."

caused much of the food to be spoiled and valuable supplies ruined. When Schuyler first arrived at the fort, in fact, he was furious to find the guards asleep.

Second in command under Schuyler was Brig. Gen. Richard Montgomery, who had fought with the British in the French and Indian Wars. Montgomery, however, felt strongly about the cause of the colonies and offered his experience and intelligence to fight the British. He had proven himself a capable leader in fighting the French, but colonial troops at Ticonderoga did not feel obligated to follow a commander other than their own.

Schuyler and Montgomery worked together well, but they had little time to prepare for a strike into Canada. Colonial agents in Quebec were sending information that Sir Guy Carleton, commander of the British forces in Canada, was planning to recapture Ticonderoga and then move south as far as he could reach—possibly even to New York City.

The two American officers quickly began to assemble equipment and supplies they would need to drive their forces into Canada. Arrangements were proceeding satisfactorily until Schuyler was called to Albany, New York, on August 17, 1775, for an important meeting with prominent regional Indian chiefs. Brigadier General Montgomery was left in command of the northern Continental army in Schuyler's absence. A scout alarmed him with the report that the British were strengthening the forts at St. Johns and elsewhere along the route that the northern army was planning to take. Furthermore, there was information that two new warships, each able to carry 20 guns, were being built in a shipyard not far from St. Johns on the Richelieu River. Montgomery decided he could not wait for orders from Schuyler, and in less than 10 days after he was given command, he was leading a force of 1,200 men on a mission to conquer half of North America for the American colonies.

Montgomery left a note for Schuyler apologizing for not waiting to consult with him, but he indicated he had acted in his best judgment when he wrote, "If I must err, let it be on the right side." When Schuyler returned two days later, ill with a fever, he was pleased with the junior officer's decision and quickly assembled 800 additional men. They set out to join Montgomery, although Schuyler himself was forced to return to Ticonderoga because of a complete collapse of his health.

Less than a month after Montgomery launched his ambitious plan to capture Quebec and win control of Canada, Benedict Arnold received approval from General Washington to lead about 1,100 of the best riflemen he could gather to the same destination—Quebec—sought by the forces from Ticonderoga. Arnold would take an eastern

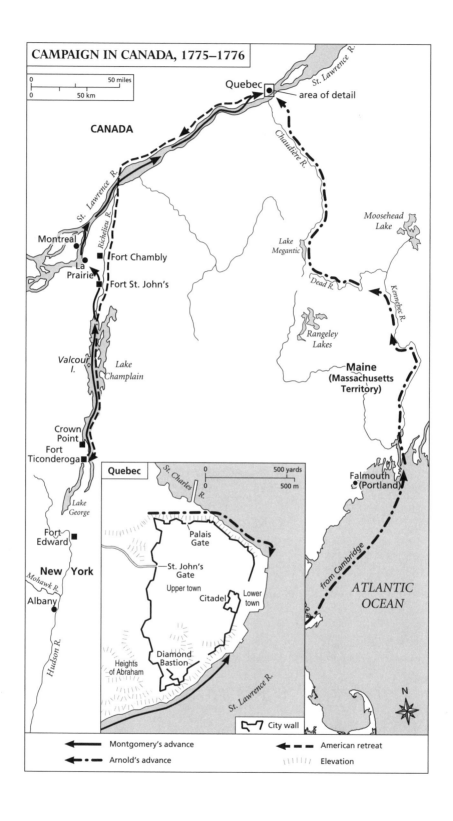

CAMPAIGN IN CANADA, 1775–1776

0   50 miles
0   50 km

St. Lawrence R.

Quebec ■ ← area of detail

St. Lawrence R.

CANADA

Chaudière R.

Montreal ●

St. Lawrence R.

■ Fort Chambly

La ● Prairie

■ Fort St. John's

Richelieu R.

Moosehead Lake

Lake Megantic

Dead R.

Kennebec R.

Valcour I.

Lake Champlain

Rangeley Lakes

Maine (Massachusetts Territory)

Crown Point ■

Fort Ticonderoga ■

Lake George

Fort Edward ■

New York

Mohawk R.

Albany ●

Hudson R.

Falmouth ● (Portland)

Quebec

St. Charles R.

0   500 yards
0   500 m

Palais Gate

St. John's Gate

Upper town

Citadel

Lower town

Diamond Bastion

Heights of Abraham

St. Lawrence R.

⌐⌐⌐ City wall

from Cambridge

ATLANTIC OCEAN

N

→ Montgomery's advance

-- → American retreat

-·→ Arnold's advance

////// Elevation

route through Maine, however, and meet Montgomery as he approached from the west and down the St. Lawrence River.

Arnold's men were devoted followers of their commander, but the task they undertook was more than they could manage. Because they started in September 1775, they were forced to contend with bitter winter weather long before they reached Quebec. The boats they used to haul food and supplies up Maine's Kennebec River and over portages were too heavy and leaky because they had been made hastily and of unseasoned wood. Much of their food was lost when the boats overturned in rapids along the rivers and streams. Men marched for miles on empty stomachs, and many of them did not survive the cold or fever brought on by their conditions. Arnold's march took twice as long as planned. Only the sheer determination and courage of the men enabled them to finally reach the fortified city of Quebec on November 8, 1775.

Montgomery's force had captured Fort St. Johns after a two-month siege and then had taken Montreal easily on November 13, but they had also encountered unexpected problems while moving down the St. Lawrence River. After the capture of Montreal, the three months' enlistment period was over for many in Montgomery's ranks, so they simply picked up their packs and headed home. Sickness and casualties from fighting at St. Johns and Montreal had also reduced the original force to a mere 400 men, about one-fourth the number that had left Ticonderoga. Arnold's troop strength had dwindled from the original 1,100 to approximately 675. Montgomery's band reached Quebec on December 2, and without delay, he began to make plans with Arnold to act quickly and complete their mission of capturing the old fortress of Quebec. Both commanders realized that the term of enlistment for many of their men was about to end on January 1. After that date, most of the remaining men could walk away or refuse to fight. The two commanders settled on December 31 as the day for the assault.

The Americans were counting heavily on surprising the city's supposedly weak defenders. Arnold and Montgomery were not prepared, however, for the arrival of a blinding snowstorm that began the night of December 30 and continued on into the next day. Despite the snow, Montgomery led his men into a position where they could overcome the guards and enter the city.

Unexpectedly, the guards were alert and watchful. One of them detected an advance party of the Americans moving toward the

The defenders of Quebec withstand the assault of Arnold and Montgomery, December 30, 1775. *(Library of Congress)*

blockhouse, where a cannon was loaded and waiting. A British officer watched as the silhouettes of the invaders appeared through the driving snow and sleet. He waited until all the Americans were within sight and then fired, killing all the colonists within range of the deadly explosion of grapeshot. One of the first to fall was Brigadier General Montgomery.

Arnold's troops in the meantime were attacking the city from the east, but they had a similar experience when Arnold himself was wounded and many of his men captured. The next move of the Americans was to lay siege to the city throughout the winter of 1776 to bring about its surrender. Although eventually 13,000 American troops were sent to Canada, there were never many more than 500 "effectives"—that is, men truly fit for fighting—against 1,600 British troops secure in Quebec. When British reinforcements arrived with the spring thaw in May, the surviving Americans slowly retreated back up the St. Lawrence. Some 5,000 Americans were left behind in Canada—dead, wounded, or captured—and another 3,000 dragged themselves back, weakened by malaria, smallpox, and dysentery; the last of the survivors did not reach safety at Fort Ticonderoga until July 1776. As it happened, this was just after the Continental Congress had made its final move toward a declaration of war against

Britain, but the grand plan of bringing Canada into the union of colonies had failed.

Within a few months the exhausted troops were put to the test again in an effort to prevent the British from capturing Fort Ticonderoga and marching south to Albany. From Albany, the redcoats would have direct access to New York City by way of the Hudson River, isolating New England from the rest of the colonies. During the summer of 1776, Arnold's men began frantically constructing a small fleet of ships in hopes of controlling Lake Champlain and protecting Ticonderoga. The British were busily building ships, and on October 11, the two fleets clashed near Valcour Island. With a total of 83 guns, the colonial ships were well armed and vigorously defended, but the experienced British easily defeated the Americans. Arnold's resistance on Lake Champlain, however, caused the British to be very cautious. As winter set in, the British commander abandoned his efforts to seize Fort Ticonderoga, and he withdrew into Canada instead of pressing down the Hudson Valley to New York City.

Both England and America recognized that control of New York City would make a crucial difference in winning the war. New York Harbor was a major gateway to Atlantic shipping, and the Hudson River connected the city to the northern frontiers. If the English occupied New York City, they would be within easy distance of New England. They would be able to move their fleet down the coast to attack any of the southern colonies, or they could use the Hudson River as a vital connector to their troops mobilizing in Canada.

After the British were forced to leave Boston in March of 1776, New York became the center of fighting for the remainder of the year. General Howe was now the supreme commander of all English forces in America, and he had the responsibility of preparing the strongest military force in the world to seize New York. For weeks after the humiliation of being driven from Boston, Howe used his time at Halifax, Nova Scotia, to make plans to attack New York. The British general was not about to move on the city until he had the assurance of an enormous advantage over the Americans in troop numbers and war supplies.

At the same time, George Washington was making plans to defend New York from attack. On March 18, 1776, the day after the evacuation from Boston, the American commander in chief ordered most of his men and weapons to hasten to New York. There were reports that Howe planned to invade the city by sea, using his warships. The American

The "Sons of Liberty" pull down the statue of George III at the Bowling Green, New York, July 1776. The lead statue was melted down to make bullets for the Continental army. *(Library of Congress, Prints & Photographs Division [LC-USZ62-2455])*

army was becoming a respectable force, at least in terms of size if not experience. Even with only the limited successes of Breed's Hill and the forced British evacuation of Boston, the colonists were feeling that they could manage the redcoats. General Washington did not have the same confidence.

THE FIRST CAMPAIGNS

Altogether about 20,000 colonials assembled around New York, making preparations during May and June for the expected attack from the sea. Men from many different colonies worked together to build earthworks to protect Long Island and Manhattan Island. By the end of June 1776, they had constructed two forts and an entire system of defense that they thought would prepare them for any British assault. At the same time that the American troops were digging in, the Second Continental Congress was meeting in nearby Philadelphia. Out of that meeting would come the Declaration of Independence.

At daybreak, on June 29, 1776, the combined fleets under Adm. Richard Howe and his brother, Gen. William Howe, began sailing into New York Harbor, one flotilla after another. Looking out his window that morning, one Patriot soldier spied "something resembling a wood of pine trees trimmed. The whole Bay was full of shipping as ever it could be. I thought all London was afloat." It was the largest concentrated naval force in British history. English warships continued to arrive during July, and by the middle of August, 32,000 British and Hessian troops were poised to strike the 20,000 Americans now in New York City.

Starting before sunrise on August 22, 1776, the British made their move. All day long, transport barges ferried about half of the invasion

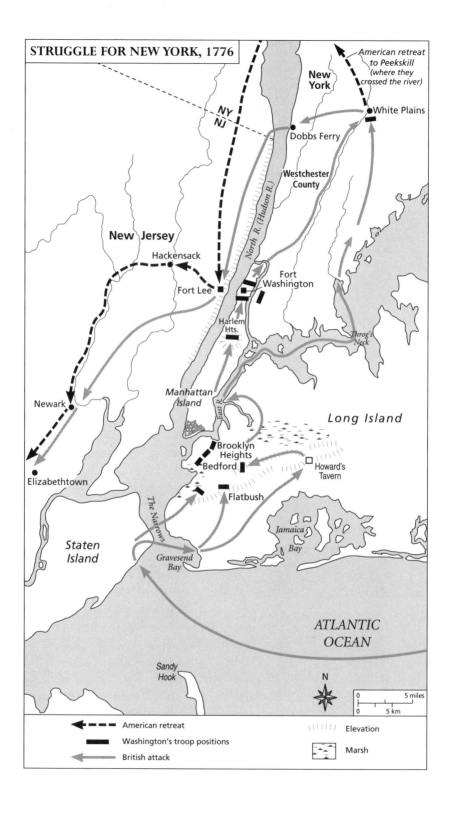

STRUGGLE FOR NEW YORK, 1776

American retreat to Peekskill (where they crossed the river)

New York

White Plains

Dobbs Ferry

Westchester County

New Jersey

Hackensack

NY
NJ

North R. (Hudson R.)

Fort Washington

Fort Lee

Harlem Hts.

Throg's Neck

Newark

Manhattan Island

East R.

Long Island

Brooklyn Heights

Bedford

Howard's Tavern

Elizabethtown

Flatbush

The Narrows

Jamaica Bay

Staten Island

Gravesend Bay

ATLANTIC OCEAN

Sandy Hook

N

0		5 miles
0		5 km

American retreat

Washington's troop positions

British attack

Elevation

Marsh

force from their encampment on Staten Island across New York Harbor to Long Island. Fortunately for the Americans, Howe had decided to land all his troops on the southeastern shore of Long Island, *behind* the Americans on Brooklyn Heights. For in spite of his preparations, General Washington had made a serious mistake in the way he had positioned his troops. The result could have meant sure destruction of the inexperienced colonial soldiers and an early end to the war.

Washington had decided not to concentrate all his men in one place. Instead, he divided them between Long Island and Manhattan Island. His strategy could have been a serious mistake if British General Howe had sailed up the East River and trapped the colonial forces on Long Island near Brooklyn Heights. The other half of Washington's army would remain helplessly on Manhattan, unable to cross the East River and join the Americans facing the enemy there. The battle at Brooklyn Heights began on the morning of August 27. The Americans were not prepared for the force of the attack, and they suffered heavy casualties in a crushing defeat.

In desperation, Washington concluded that he must try to salvage his remaining forces on Long Island. He must somehow get them across the East River to join the other half of his army on Manhattan Island. The only reason he was lucky enough to still have that choice was that General Howe remembered the battle at Breed's Hill very well. In spite of the major rebel defeat on Long Island, Howe halted the final attacks on Brooklyn Heights to give his men time to dig themselves in. If he had given the order to press forward and capture the trapped Americans, he might have ended the war then and there.

The prospects for Washington's evacuation plans were dismal, since the Americans had no large transport boats as the British did to ferry them across the river. Washington knew, also, that he must prevent the British from discovering the attempt to evacuate. It was John Glover of Marblehead, Massachusetts, who offered a solution. An experienced mariner, Glover had been appointed by the Continental Congress to head the infant American navy. In a moment of sheer heroism, he and Israel Hutchinson of Salem devised a plan to use every available small boat they could find to ferry as many of the trapped soldiers as possible from Long Island across the East River to Manhattan. Glover's Marbleheaders and Hutchinson's Twenty-seventh Massachusetts unit were coastal fishermen who knew how to manage small boats in rough waters. Throughout the night of August 29, their rugged oarsmen pulled their loaded boats through rain and blinding fog. For six hours nonstop, they crossed the East River back and forth. When the British awoke the morning of August 30, they were astonished to find the Americans were completely gone from Brooklyn Heights. The escape had been orderly and a total success. Military strategists still regard the American escape from Long Island as a masterful achievement.

The Americans had lost Long Island, but they still had an army. Inexperience and terror had caused many of the Patriot foot soldiers to run during the battle for Long Island, but their commander, General Washington, did not show any of his own alarm. His outward steadiness and determination gave heart to his men, but there was growing uncertainty among many of the troops who had felt so confident just a few days earlier. Suddenly, the Americans faced the prospect of a long war full of bitter fighting. Long Island was not like Breed's Hill at all. In the Battle of Long Island, the British did not give the Americans time to reload their muskets. The colonists were terrified as the enemy charged with bayonets and either ran them through or sent them fleeing.

After the panic he saw in his men on Long Island, Washington was worried about how much he could count on them under fire. He faced

The Battle of Long Island, August 27, 1776 *(National Archives, Still Pictures Branch, NWDNS-111-SC-96741)*

a risky choice—to stand and fight to save New York (Manhattan) or to continue a calculated retreat. One of his advisers counseled him to abandon Manhattan immediately and escape to Westchester County, just to the north of the city. Another recommendation was to burn New York and leave nothing for the British. After days of indecision, Washington finally decided to leave Manhattan on September 15, 1776, without setting fire to the city.

If it had not been for the feebleness of General Howe's pursuit, Washington's troops probably would have all been captured, and the army destroyed. This was the second time Howe lost a perfect chance to sweep vigorously toward victory and end the barely-begun American revolution.

A short time after the Americans evacuated Manhattan Island, a great fire broke out in New York, and almost one-fourth of the city burned. On the day after the fire, a young American schoolteacher from Connecticut, Nathan Hale, was "taken up and dragged without ceremony to the execution post and hung up." Hale had volunteered to slip back into the city to gather information and had been imprisoned as a spy when caught making suspicious drawings. It was easy to accuse this American patriot of starting the sweeping fires in the city after the rebel retreat, and upon the gallows, Hale made his brief but memorable farewell: "I only regret that I have but one life to lose for my country."

General Washington moved his army to White Plains, New York, but he had been reluctant to abandon Manhattan Island altogether. Eventually some 4,600 American troops were positioned around Fort Washington at the northern tip of the island, a decision that led to disaster, for it was not long before the British overran the fort. Lost were priceless weapons and other supplies, but the most serious consequence was the death (53), wounding (250), or capture (2,818) of more than 3,000 American soldiers. The British now held all of New York's Long Island and Manhattan Island and would keep them for the remainder of the war.

Even though the Americans had fought courageously on some days, the overall campaign to hold New York had been a slow but inevitable retreat. Washington was able to escape into New Jersey with most of his army intact by the time winter arrived, but the prospects for the Americans seemed almost hopeless. A British officer who followed the retreat was shocked that "many of the Rebels who were killed were without

Nathan Hale, immortal-
ized in marble, faces
execution by the British,
September 21, 1776.
(Library of Congress)

shoes or Stockings, without any proper shirt or Waistcoat, also in great want of blankets. They must suffer extremely." He could not imagine how the Americans could continue fighting this way, so he had every reason to believe that the American rebellion would soon end. He did not understand, however, that the Americans now had more than their pride at stake. They were fighting for a new ideal—their full independence from England.

6

RING OUT LIBERTY!

Many of the American soldiers who retreated from New York had first started fighting in April 1775 at Lexington and Concord. They had survived the battle at Breed's Hill and then had entered the freed city of Boston with their new commander in chief, George Washington. That first 12 months of combat, from April 1775 to March 1776, was not especially a war of independence in their minds. They were fighting to make a point, to send a message to England that they would not be bullied into absolute obedience to unfair English laws and decisions, even if it meant sacrifice and bloodshed. By the time they marched out of Boston in August 1776 into the battle arena of New York City, however, a change had occurred in the men of the new Continental army. They had celebrated the Declaration of Independence (announced on July 4, 1776) and knew that there was no turning back. They would now be struggling to become citizens of free and independent states, a very different thing from just trying to get the British to back down. Now there was a cause to fight for!

The Second Continental Congress had met in May 1775 in Philadelphia as planned the year before, but it did not complete its main achievement until more than a year later, in July 1776. The delegates began by anxiously debating the consequences of the rapid-fire events of the spring of 1775. With the fighting at Lexington and Concord, the surprise seizure of Ticonderoga, and the valiant defense at Breed's Hill, many colonial representatives concluded that a war had already begun, without a declaration of war. They were unsure about the responsibility and authority of the congress, but the question most urgently needing

Mount Vernon, George Washington's estate in Virginia, was a mark of his wealth and prominence. *(Library of Congress, Prints & Photographs Division [LC-USZ62-1237])*

an answer was simple: What should the colonies do next? With Washington's troops on the march toward New York, should they make the final move toward independence or should they try to repair the damage in their relations with Britain? Was there still a chance for peace?

Some of the more cautious colonial leaders such as Joseph Galloway of Pennsylvania did not attend the Second Continental Congress. Others present were entirely dedicated to the cause of independence, among them Benjamin Franklin of Pennsylvania and Thomas Jefferson of Virginia. The well-known and wealthy Boston Patriot John Hancock was elected president of the congress. With the urgency of military events unfolding, John Adams urged the immediate appointment of a commander for the hundreds of volunteer troops camped outside Boston. Adams particularly wanted the congress to name a general from the southern colonies to give Britain a clear message: The colonies were united.

Tall, handsome George Washington of Virginia attended the congress in uniform, prepared immediately to join the action in New England. He was everyone's choice for general—a wealthy gentleman from a powerful southern colony, a self-disciplined and determined soldier, and an unselfish man of high moral character. In 1774, men close to Washington said he had made his position evident: "If the English should attack the People of Boston, he would raise a thousand Men at his own expense and march at their head to New England to their aid."

Washington was elected unanimously to serve as commander in chief of the Continental army, and he immediately announced that he would serve without pay, although he expected to be reimbursed for expenses. Placed under his command were four major generals: Artemas Ward, Israel Putnam, Charles Lee, and Philip Schuyler. Leaving the

George Washington (1732–99) *(Library of Congress)*

Second Continental Congress in June 1775 for Boston soon after his appointment, General Washington considered the effect on the colonial position of the capture of Fort Ticonderoga and the securing of Lake Champlain. On his journey to Boston, he was stopped by a jubilant courier adding the surprising news of the valiant defense of Breed's Hill on June 17, 1775. Organizing a Continental army was an urgent task.

Washington's new Continental army, however, was still, technically speaking, an English one. No official break with Britain had been made, and members of the Second Continental Congress struggled to defend the creation of this army. As an explanation, John Dickinson and Thomas Jefferson created the "Declaration on the Causes of Taking Up Arms," and the approved declaration was then sent by the congress to England in July 1775. "We mean not to dissolve this union which has so long and so happily subsisted between us. . . . We have not raised armies with ambitious designs of separation from Great Britain, and establishing independent States," it read in part.

John Dickinson of Pennsylvania was a Quaker strongly opposed to violence. No one could ever accuse him of being less than a faithful British subject. Back in 1767 he had written the famous *Letters from a Pennsylvania Farmer,* which first appeared in a series in a newspaper and later were published as a pamphlet. The *Letters* firmly supported colonial loyalty to Britain but just as firmly rejected the British right to tax the colonies at will. Opposing English taxes was one thing, but to go to war with Britain was too extreme a step for Dickinson. John Dickinson represented many people, especially from the Middle Colonies of Pennsylvania, Maryland, Delaware, New York, and New Jersey. They were increasingly angered by England's oppression, but actually to break with England was unthinkable. Surely there were still ways to resolve things.

The image of a dove carrying an olive branch was a traditional symbol of peace, taken from the Bible. An "Olive Branch" petition was written by Dickinson in 1775 after the battles at Concord and Breed's Hill, urgently begging the king to stop all military action and to work with the congress toward peaceful solutions. Approved by the Second Continental Congress, it was delivered in August 1775 by the grandson of the great William Penn. When King George III stubbornly refused even to receive it, he closed the door on the last hope of compromise for some Continental Congress delegates.

Colonial leaders knew they had support from some in the British Parliament who urged that all British troops be withdrawn from the

Thomas Paine
(1737–1809)
(Library of Congress)

colonies. Leaders in Parliament, among them Edmund Burke and John Wilkes, repeatedly stood to defend the rights of the American rebels. Even Lord North, the weak and pompous British prime minister, brought plans for a peaceful resolution to the conflict to Parliament in July 1775. A modified resolution was finally adopted, allowing some recognition to the colonial Continental Congress. In another example of terrible timing, however, Parliament at the same time created another act to punish the colonies. This one would cut off all trade and commerce between England and the 13 American colonies. It would begin March 1, 1776. In spite of Edmund Burke's brilliant speech in Parliament condemning it, the trade act passed in December of 1775, canceling any good accomplished by the North resolution.

While efforts by men like John Dickinson urged moderation and careful thought, others in the colonies worked energetically to persuade people differently. A little booklet appeared in January 1776 in Philadelphia, titled *Common Sense,* which used words easily understood by everyone. Just one month after Parliament voted to cut off all trade with the American colonies, Quaker writer Thomas Paine attacked the Parliament, everything British, and especially the king in shrill words. "O ye that love mankind, stand forth. . . . Ye that dare oppose not only the tyranny but the tyrant, stand forth!" wrote Paine. The radical booklet was read eagerly in the colonies, just as Dickinson's

Letters from a Pennsylvania Farmer had been nine years before. Paine's words, however, called for a much stronger stand than the *Letters* did. On his final page, Paine declared in simple and stark type: "The Free and Independent States of America."

At precisely the same time that Paine was rallying some colonists to revolution, others were secretly taking small but critical steps to find military support for the Continental army and the tiny navy. Surprisingly, the source they turned to was France. Although France had been the enemy of the English colonists for decades, what other country would now be more interested in humbling the great British Empire? Well-known and respected by Europeans, Benjamin Franklin and two other Patriots were dispatched to France to seek aid. While the French offered the Americans large amounts of sympathy and moral support, they were not yet ready to agree to an alliance. Such a move would

put them immediately at war with England, and besides, what if the American revolutionary movement failed utterly? They would be made to look foolish again. So the French agreed to provide supplies and financial support in secret, while remaining publicly neutral. It was a great disappointment to Franklin and the Continental Congress.

Independence Hall in Philadelphia served as the meeting place for the Continental Congress. *(National Archives, Still Pictures Branch, NWDNS-66-G-1E-6)*

The Continental Congress continued to meet on and off throughout the year, gathering back in Philadelphia when there was specific work to be done. Otherwise, congress members returned home to tend to their families and businesses. When the congress reconvened in the blistering heat of June 1776, "independence" was on the lips of the delegates. It had now been more than a year since the events at Lexington and Concord and Breed's Hill. Aid from France was not yet assured. General Washington had finally pressured the British to evacuate their troops from Boston at the end of March, but now the British were threatening to close down New York Harbor. Meanwhile, 900 Patriots had defeated a Loyalist uprising in the south. It was a roller coaster of events—but still not a declared revolution.

Richard Henry Lee had arrived in Philadelphia in early June with a "resolution for independence" from Virginia's House of Burgesses members, hoping for approval. Clear and strong, it asserted that "these United Colonies are, and of right ought to be, free and independent states." The time had come for a decision. All the representatives were convinced that if the resolution passed, it must be unanimous. Anything less would undermine the military effort and allow an objecting colony to provide a safe retreat for the British. Could the "crazy quilt" of colonies agree?

Knowing in advance that the resolution would be presented, each colony had voted in its own assembly whether or not to support it. Representatives had thus come to this session of the Continental Congress carrying their assemblies' decisions. Some delegations were divided, and some individuals attending represented only themselves. The Pennsylvania assembly was solidly opposed to a total break with Britain, but their delegation included one member who was determined to speak out for independence—none other than Benjamin Franklin. Delaware had three representatives, two for independence, one against, but Caesar Rodney, one of the two favoring such a resolution, had not yet arrived in Philadelphia. With John Hancock of Massachusetts presiding over the meetings with energy and dignity, the congress determined that all discussion about independence would be held in secret until a firm and unanimous decision was reached.

Richard Henry Lee presented the Virginia resolution for declaring independence on June 7, and it was soon clear that the delegates were too divided to come to any clear decision. Instead, on June 10, the congress did what all such groups do in such circumstances: postponed any vote for three weeks and appointed a committee. This special committee was to "prepare a Declaration to the effect of the said . . . resolution." The committee consisted of John Adams, Benjamin Franklin, Thomas

Jefferson, Robert R. Livingston, and Roger Sherman, and since Jefferson had received the most votes, he became the chairman. It was also agreed that he would write the basic draft of a declaration of independence that would support the Virginia resolution.

Only 33 years old, Jefferson was already known and respected by men of influence throughout the colonies. A modest, intelligent, and extremely private person, he was seen as thoughtful and wise beyond his years. He had read many books and discussed countless ideas related to political freedom, and he would draw on his years of reading and thinking as he proceeded to work away, night and day, in his boarding-house room there in Philadelphia. One of his favored influences was the English philosopher John Locke (1632–1704), who had written in 1690 that God had granted people certain rights, including "life, liberty, and the ownership of property." When rulers refused to guarantee and protect those rights, people had a right and duty to find other rulers. Jefferson agreed with Locke but was uncomfortable with the emphasis on property, so he changed that to "pursuit of happiness."

After Jefferson completed his first rough draft, he showed it to three other members of the committee, and they suggested some additions and revisions (most fairly minor). The fifth member, 75-year-old Benjamin Franklin, was sick in bed, but the revised version was brought to him, and he made a few more changes. Jefferson then made three "fair copies" of the revised declaration in his own handwriting and presented one to the secretary of the congress on June 28. The Second Continental Congress could no longer avoid the challenge of considering the idea of independence.

When the debate began on July 1, the issue was simply whether to adopt the Virginia resolution to declare independence. In the weeks since June 10, the congress had been voting on many matters having to do with the ongoing war against Britain, but many of the delegates were still opposed to making a complete break with the homeland. John Dickinson of Pennsylvania made an eloquent plea for patience, at least until aid from France was assured. Then it was the turn of John Adams of Massachusetts to speak. He did not consider himself a powerful public speaker like Patrick Henry or a profound thinker like Thomas Jefferson. But Adams spoke with intelligence, intensity, and conviction, and some representatives would later give him credit for being the "Atlas of Independence," who persuaded them to vote for the resolution.

Drafting the Declaration of Independence (*left to right*: Franklin, Jefferson, Livingston, Adams, Sherman), June 1776 (*Library of Congress*)

An unofficial vote late on July 1 made it clear that there was not total support for the resolution, so the official vote was postponed until the next day. Meanwhile, a messenger rode on horseback to Caesar Rodney in Delaware to urge his attendance, and Rodney rode frantically through pouring rain to be present on July 2 when the resolution came up for a formal vote. After more debate, those who had resisted taking such a drastic step began to come around, even if somewhat reluctantly. With New York's delegation abstaining (because it still lacked instructions from its own assembly), the rest of the colonies unanimously adopted the Virginia resolution for independence. (Some, John Adams included, have argued that this July 2 vote was Americans' true "declaration of independence.")

The next order of business was to consider the formal declaration that Jefferson and his committee had been working on, but as it was late in the day, the first reading of that document was put off until the next day. Hearing the declaration read aloud for the first time on the morning of July 3, some representatives objected to the inflammatory language, but they agreed on the basic ideas. The congress then examined the document sentence by sentence. The list of complaints against the king was finally approved—except for one. On this issue, representatives were soon standing on chairs, trying to be heard, and some were even threatening to reject the declaration altogether.

Among his charges against the king, Jefferson had written: "He has waged cruel war against human nature itself, violating its most sacred rights of life and liberty in the persons of a distant people, who never offended him, captivating and carrying them into slavery in another hemisphere." He wrote on about "the warfare of the Christian king of Great Britain, determined to keep open a market where MEN should be bought and sold." For some 150 years, African people had been captured and delivered by ship to the American colonies for sale as slaves. Some southern colonies had many more African slaves than English people. Yet most of the colonies disliked slavery and wished it would end. Both Benjamin Franklin and Thomas Jefferson felt strongly that slavery must end. John Adams came to Jefferson's defense, claiming that slavery could not be accepted if "all men

Thomas Jefferson observes the work of one of his slaves at Monticello, his Virginia plantation. *(Library of Congress)*

Slavery throughout the Colonies

WHEN THE AMERICAN REVOLUTION BEGAN, SLAVERY was already a profitable business in the colonies. Although the first African slaves had been introduced into Virginia and other southern colonies, Massachusetts was the first American colony to make trading in human lives legal.

The interest in chattel slavery (the practice of owning human beings) began with a need for inexpensive labor. A farmer in Connecticut, for instance, might recognize, after a few years of clearing land and expanding the size of his acreage, that he could become an even bigger landholder if he simply had more help. European immigrants often served as indentured servants, contracted to work for a period of time, usually seven years. Afterward they were given some money and perhaps tools to start their own life. This was one option for cheap labor for the colonial farmer, but owning slaves was even more attractive. Since slaves were considered as property, not as human beings, a farmer could treat them much as he would a horse or a mule.

The first slaves in the American colonies, in fact, were not Africans but American Indians. Before long, this practice of capturing and selling American Indians spread throughout the colonies. Native people, however, made poor slaves; they refused to work, sickened, worked slowly and ineffectively, or knowing the area, simply fled into the forests. American slave traders eventually turned to the more risky and expensive African slave trade for cheap labor. By the 1750s, there were 25,000 white residents in the South, compared to 40,000 black slaves and 60,000 Creek, Cherokee, Choctaw, and Chickasaw slaves.

Many of the earliest slave ships were built in Massachusetts and other New England shipyards. Much of the early wealth accumulated by Bostonians and other New England families came from the slave trade. By 1775, there were approximately 60,000 slaves in the New England colonies and some 450,000 in the southern colonies. The colonial dream of independence did not include freedom for the American slaves.

are created equal." The South Carolina and Georgia delegations were furious. Either this section was taken out of the declaration or they would vote against it. To keep unity in the congress and in the eyes of the world, the offending section was removed from the document.

RING OUT LIBERTY!

The signing of the Declaration of Independence, July 4, 1776 *(Library of Congress)*

By early evening of July 4, the members of the congress had completed their editing of the version submitted by Jefferson and his committee. They had made 40 changes, had cut away some 25 percent of the text, and—with some exceptions—had subtly improved the original. John Hancock called for the vote and (with New York again abstaining) approval was unanimous. Hancock signed the edited document with his distinctive flourish, and Charles Taylor, secretary of the congress, also signed as a witness; not until August 2 or later would the other delegates to the congress sign the Declaration of Independence. The edited document was then taken at once to a Philadelphia printer, John Dunlop, who worked throughout the night and printed numerous copies that were then sent by horseback, stagecoach, and ship to the different states and army leaders.

Word of the bold decisions of the Continental Congress soon spread throughout Philadelphia, and the citizens began to decorate their city with the so-called Grand Union flags—13 red and white stripes (representing the 13 colonies) stitched next to the British Union Jack. (It would be June 1777 before the congress adopted the flag that replaced the Union Jack with the circle of 13 stars on a field of blue.) On July 8, as the "liberty bell" of the State House tower began to ring steadily, crowds

George Washington oversees the first public reading of the Declaration of Independence in New York City, July 9, 1776. *(Library of Congress, Prints & Photographs Division [LC-USZ62-96106])*

gathered to hear the first public reading of the Declaration of Independence. Its words were not all that surprising to these Philadelphians, for they simply set forth ideas they already believed in, rights they had always had as English citizens. But when the reader came to the list of complaints against the king, loud cheers greeted each accusation. The British coat of arms over the State House door was pulled down as a final gesture, and rejoicing continued through that day and into the night.

The very next day, Gen. George Washington had the Declaration read to units of his army then stationed on Manhattan Island. That evening, the Sons of Liberty pulled down the gilded equestrian statue of King George III that had stood in lower Manhattan. In the days and weeks that followed, public readings and celebrations of the Declaration of Independence took place throughout the new "States of America." Not all Americans, however, were convinced that declaring independence was the right thing to do. They recognized that the adoption of the Declaration of Independence was also a declaration of war against England.

The Declaration of Independence offered a bold and persuasive defense of the radical break that the American colonies were finally prepared to make. It would also serve in the centuries that followed to inspire other peoples seeking to declare independence from their rulers. But in July 1776, that was the furthest thing from the minds of those who had composed and adopted this document. The most pressing issue was not some abstract notion of liberty but a very real one: how to defeat the most powerful nation of the day. As the struggle for independence now formally began, it appeared to many that the American colonists had foolishly entered a war they had little chance of winning.

7

WASHINGTON IN CHARGE

With his new army of poorly supplied and undisci-plined militiamen, Washington had made many mistakes in trying to hold New York City and had failed. General Howe, on the other hand, with all the gathered strength of the British navy and army, had lost one of the greatest opportunities to end the American Revolution almost before it started. He failed to pursue and capture Washington's army as it retreated into New Jersey that November of 1776. Even though the Continental army was in desperate retreat in the face of great British strength, the memory of the battle at Charlestown's Breed's Hill haunted General Howe. Throughout the war, Howe would remember the savage defense of their fortified position by the ragged colonial sol-diers and would fear that it would happen again. By salvaging his exhausted forces, Washington was able to regroup and add to his army, thereby continuing the war.

As Washington's troops scrambled in retreat, the British were delighted with the prize they knew they held in New York City, which remained in their hands throughout the war. It became indispensable as the base for nearly all their military efforts in the colonies. New York City was also the major Loyalist stronghold in the colonies, and the grateful citizens provided a congenial and even festive environment for the British troops. At the same time, Patriot troops were suffering from lack of many simple comforts like decent food and warm clothing. No wonder the British were certain the colonies could be brought to their knees within a year.

Charles, Lord
Cornwallis 1738–1805)
(Library of Congress)

When Washington had a chance in November 1776 to assess the damage to his army, he found it had shrunk from 18,000 to about 5,000 men. Hundreds of colonial soldiers had deserted during the haphazard and frantic New York campaigns, many had been killed or wounded, and 5,000 others had been captured by the British. From the time of his appointment as commander in chief back in June 1775, Washington had not won a single battle. At this early point in the war, it seemed to most colonists and to Washington himself that the American Revolution was surely doomed.

When forced out of New York, the Continental army barely escaped pursuit by British general Charles, Lord Cornwallis. Cornwallis was not like the overly cautious General Howe; he was determined to destroy the few remaining men devoted to Washington. Howe, though, commanded him to wait for the main army to provide support. Washington took

George Washington crossing the Delaware *(National Archives, Still Pictures Branch, NWDNS-66-G-15D[25])*

advantage of the additional time, crossed the Delaware River, and once again barely escaped with his men, this time into Pennsylvania.

Careful to destroy any boats they did not take with them in crossing the Delaware, the Americans managed to delay any pursuit by the enemy. Nevertheless, the Continental army faced an overwhelming dis-

advantage. Even though troop reinforcements arrived from Fort Ticonderoga and nearby Philadelphia, Washington could count only 6,000 men. Furthermore, one of his senior officers, Charles Lee, had been captured just outside New York City, and others were too distant to come to his aid. Once again, the Americans were in a state of disarray. Washington admitted in a letter, kept secret at the time, that without more men, "the game will be pretty well up."

After escaping into Pennsylvania, Washington had no grand strategy for reversing his losses, but he recognized the importance of winning even a small victory to boost the morale of his men. As Christmas of 1776 drew near, the British were comfortably quartered in New York City. The American army, meanwhile, was surviving snow and freezing temperatures by huddling around open campfires west of Trenton. Soldiers wrapped their scabby feet in old shirts and cooked spoiled meat to survive. The commander in chief described some of them as being "entirely naked and most so thinly clad as to be unfit for service."

Despite the condition of his men, Washington counted on tactical mistakes made by General Howe. The British commander assumed that the Americans would be too demoralized to fight in the bitter winter conditions. With this assumption, Howe arranged for a few of his men to occupy quarters in towns south and west of New York. Howe himself, in the meantime, remained comfortably with most of the British army in New York City.

One of the New Jersey cities that served as a British outpost guarding New York City was Trenton. The men assigned to stay there through the winter were the Hessian mercenaries. Throughout the evening of December 25, the stone barracks in Trenton were dry, warm, and festive as the German mercenary soldiers celebrated Christmas. There was laughter and plenty to eat and drink. Just across the river and downstream, about 10 miles away, General Washington was calling on his exhausted and dispirited troops to be brave a little longer. Washington's plan was to ferry an attack force across the treacherous Delaware River during the night of December 25 and catch the groggy Hessians unprepared. It would have been a risky venture even in ideal weather, but the river was full of floating sheets of ice, much of it in slabs weighing tons and moving at speeds capable of smashing the ferrying boats to splinters.

The same men who had rescued the stranded troops on Long Island, John Glover's Marbleheaders, rowed back and forth across the river. They carried not only troops but cannon and teams of horses to a site about nine miles below Trenton. In one of the clumsy boats, urging his men on, was General Washington. One of the best-known paintings of American history would later capture this moment when Washington stood in his boat to lead his men. Straining with his oar in the bow of the boat in the painting is Prince Whipple, the African-American aide to General Whipple.

The Americans did not catch the enemy completely by surprise—there was one guard sober enough to detect the rush of bayonet-wielding infantrymen. It was too late, however, for the rest of the drowsy Hessians to defend themselves. In less than one hour, Washington and his ragged men captured 900 of the enemy and some desperately needed provisions. The swift victory raised the spirits of the Americans. It was especially important because they had succeeded in launching an attack, not just repelling the enemy, and they had used an unfamiliar weapon with deadly force—the bayonet.

Washington, meanwhile, feared he would not be able to keep this part of the Continental army intact. The period of enlistment for many of the men was running out, and the commander would be forced once again to work with inexperienced recruits. To Washington's surprise, though, many of the men agreed to stay on for another six weeks, making it possible to meet the British head-on for a second time in the course of less than 10 days. This time the confrontation would occur at Princeton, New Jersey.

As soon as General Cornwallis learned about the surprise attack on Trenton, he rushed 8,000 well-equipped and well-rested British regulars to punish Washington. Meanwhile, the American general had made the hazardous crossing of the Delaware to the Trenton side once again. Washington's confidence had improved when most of his men agreed to continue with the struggle instead of going home early. The Americans were in good spirits and ready to press on, but there were only 5,000 of them, and they were still fighting hunger and fatigue. Washington was unaware of the presence of Cornwallis until it was too late for him to escape back across the river into Pennsylvania. The Americans appeared hopelessly trapped by the British, who would be merciless in their determination to get even for their humiliation at Trenton. Instead of confronting the British directly, the rebels decided to try and slip away from the enemy in the middle of the night.

The temperature had fallen steadily throughout the day of January 2, freezing all the mud and water in the roads. During the night of January 3, the Continental army slipped through the grasp of the British one more time. While a few unselfish men remained in the American camp feeding fires and making as much noise as they could to trick the British, the entire remaining American force quietly escaped. They managed to transport their guns and supplies by wrapping the wagon wheels in rags. The road Washington's men took was newly laid out, and men and horses crippled themselves as they stumbled over stumps not yet removed from the roadbed. One man among the long line of escaping troops wrote,

> . . . when ordered forward again, one, two or three men in each platoon would stand, with their arms supported, fast asleep; a platoon next in rear advancing on them . . . they, in walking . . . would strike a stub and fall.

When the sun came up, the American escape was nearly complete, but a British officer sighted rebels moving toward a strategic bridge on the road outside Princeton and quickly moved in two brigades to attack. Soon the fighting became a blur of confusion, and there was the

Camp Life for Colonial Troops

IT WAS A LUCKY SOLDIER WHO WAS CAMPED NEAR home during the Revolutionary War. He could send home his homespun hunting shirt for cleaning and mending, request new blankets and socks, beg for vegetables and fruit, and relish the sugar and coffee sent from home. Otherwise this same soldier suffered continually from an inadequate diet. He was dependent on army rations and greatly overpriced local foods purchased by his officers, if any could be found. In the earliest days of the war, most soldiers served close to home. But even these soldiers learned to bring their own weapons and homey necessities: scissors, needles, writing tools, dice, a folding knife and fork, fishhook and line, a sundial compass.

When the troops were not on the move, officers put them to work building fortifications, digging trenches, and practicing maneuvers. For cooking and heat, a soldier scoured the countryside for fence posts and even cut green trees. He often went without shoes, slept on a scattering of straw in a tent or rough log hut, and drank foul water. Blackflies, mosquitoes, and lice were his companions.

The soldier was probably often sick, either with dysentery from bad water, from too much gin, or, worse, from the smallpox epidemics that would sweep through camps. A colonel who recovered from smallpox requested discharge from "this Retreating, Raged, Starved, lousey, thevish Pockey Army in this unhealthy Country." In 1776, at least 20 percent of Washington's troops had dysentery all the time. Barns, tents, and rough log barracks were filled with the sick. In desperation, Washington required all of his troops to be inoculated against smallpox, then a new and unpredictable procedure. At the end of the war, General Washington showed his respect and gratitude in official public statements to his now hardened and skilled soldiers who had served faithfully through much hardship and deprivation.

prospect that the Americans would run. At the height of the crisis, General Washington himself, astride his mount, thrust into the thickest of the battle and directed his soldiers. An attendant to the general was afraid he would witness his commander's certain death, but Washington emerged untouched. He had inspired his men; the Americans did not retreat but won decisively. These New Jersey victories were crucial at a time when the British were convinced that the colonies were about to collapse. Against a better prepared and better equipped army, Washington had gambled and won. He had kept the War for Independence alive.

The victories at Trenton and Princeton enabled the Americans to end the retreat that had begun four months earlier in August 1776 on Long Island. After the battle of Princeton, Washington found a suitable winter refuge for his dwindling army at Morristown, New Jersey. Winter was relatively kind to the Continental army while it regrouped at Morristown. During the remaining winter and early spring months of 1777, Washington concentrated on improving the morale and health of his men, many of whom were afflicted with the deadly disease of smallpox. Refusing to yield to despair, the American commander built isolation quarters for the stricken men. To avoid the problem of boredom, he directed the healthy troops to construct a fort, later called Fort Nonsense. By May, the main body of the Continental army at Morristown was well on its way to recovery. It had survived the winter and was, in fact, stronger than it had been before Trenton and Princeton. The bloodiest fighting, however, then shifted farther north to Lake Champlain, while Washington remained with the main army in Morristown.

While American troops were busy in New Jersey during the winter of 1776 and 1777, the Continental Congress continued its urgent efforts to find aid and support from foreign countries for the infant United States. In September 1776, experienced diplomats Silas Deane, Benjamin Franklin, and Arthur Lee were appointed to make treaties of trade and friendship with European countries; these treaties would allow the colonies to borrow desperately needed money. By December 1776, the three men began their task in Paris. In March 1777, on the heels of Washington's morale-building victories at Trenton and Princeton, the Continental Congress appointed several other special diplomats. Their task was to offer attractive deals such as fishing grounds and pieces of North American territory to several countries, Spain and France in particular. Perhaps they could be persuaded to declare war on Britain.

By the end of August 1777, General Howe had transported his army to the head of Chesapeake Bay. From there he planned to march about 70 miles northward into Philadelphia, the seat of the new American government. This move to occupy Philadelphia turned into another major blunder by the British. General Howe was originally part of a three-pronged campaign devised by Gen. John Burgoyne. A most unlikely character—something of a playboy as well as a playwright, and known as "Gentleman Johnny"—Burgoyne had managed to get himself promoted to general and then, in 1777, got the British government to adopt his plan to defeat the Americans. Burgoyne's goal was to divide and conquer the colonies once and for all by isolating troublesome New England. Burgoyne himself would lead a large force out of Canada, down Lake Champlain, toward Albany. Colonel St. Leger would meet him there, marching from Lake Ontario in the west, along the Mohawk Valley.

In his part of the plan, General Howe was expected to leave New York City and bring his troops up the Hudson River Valley to Albany. Howe instead received permission from London, without Burgoyne's knowledge, to march on Philadelphia. He was convinced that by conquering the American capital, he would bring a swift end to the war for independence. Also, Howe was confident he could take Philadelphia and still have time to proceed up the Hudson to unite with Burgoyne and St. Leger in Albany. Howe's deviation from Burgoyne's plans was a fatal mistake that eventually cost him his command.

Before he entered Philadelphia in September 1777, Howe clashed with the Americans in a bitter battle alongside a lazy stream called Brandywine Creek. Washington's army was not prepared for Howe's flanking maneuver, a tactic he had used to smash the Continentals in the battle of Long Island. This time, however, the American recruits were not so easily terrified; even though they were forced to retreat, they did so in an orderly way. Edward Hector, a black artilleryman, typified the Americans' determination when he calmly refused to abandon his valuable cargo of ammunition. Under heavy fire, he saved his wagon load and team of horses. The Battle of Brandywine Creek on September 11, 1777, was another defeat for the Americans, but only on the field. Morale remained high, and General Washington reported to the Continental Congress, "Notwithstanding the misfortune of the day, I am happy to find the troops in good spirits." He added, "I hope another time we shall compensate for the losses now sustained."

One of the casualties of Brandywine Creek was the marquis de Lafayette, who took a bullet in the thigh. He was not long in recovering, however. More serious was the loss of confidence in General Washington by some of his senior officers and members of congress. They had begun to doubt the general's ability to successfully lead the American army. Washington knew men were talking about replacing him, but he did not show his concern and continued on despite the doubts and rumors.

Instead of lamenting the disappointing loss at Brandywine Creek, Washington met with his staff of officers and began secretly making

John Burgoyne
(1722–92)
(Library of Congress)

plans for the most ambitious offensive yet undertaken by the Americans. Most of the British strength was concentrated around a little town that would later become a part of Philadelphia—Germantown. Philadelphia was already lost to the enemy, but perhaps the Continental army could strike at the heart of the British and Hessian strength in a bold, unexpected attack. This would raise the spirits of the Americans while making a proud statement of defiance to the enemy.

On paper, the Americans' strategy for attacking Germantown looked workable—but the battle did not go as planned. After surprising the British with an ambush launched at dawn on October 4, 1777, nearly 3,000 Continentals fought with a new confidence and threatened to overwhelm the sluggish enemy. General Howe, tardy as usual, thought the attack was coming from a mere scouting party until he felt the explosion of shot from American cannon. The Americans' assault began to weaken, however, when fog made it difficult to identify the redcoats. Some of Washington's troops even mistakenly fired on each other. Suddenly the troops were facing a shortage of ammunition, and by late in the day, the Continental army was forced into retreat.

General Howe marched his troops into Philadelphia for the winter, but capture of the American capital had no effect whatever on the

American resolve to continue fighting. Unlike European capitals, the new American capital was not the entrenched center of national life and identity. The Continental Congress simply moved to York, about 100 miles west of Philadelphia. Meanwhile, Howe's march to Philadelphia ruined General Burgoyne's plans to meet at Albany. The grand strategy of isolating New England was in trouble.

General Washington was not dismayed, despite the loss of Germantown. American losses were heavy (about 1,000 men), but there had been none of the panic that had sent men running in the Long Island campaign and made it such a disaster. Other countries in Europe, in fact, were impressed by the determination and scrappiness of the Continental army. France, in particular, was attentive to the growing strength of the young American army. Since December 1776, Benjamin Franklin had been in France on behalf of the American colonies, working to get French aid for the cause of independence. Now that there were some American successes to strengthen these attempts, France's interest increased. When Benjamin Franklin again met with the French government in Paris, in December 1777 and in January 1778, there was good reason to hope that Britain's old enemy would soon take sides with the Americans.

At the same time that Washington's army was beginning to achieve an identity, the Second Continental Congress was struggling during the summer and fall of 1777 to create a more permanent government. It was difficult to reach agreement on how much authority this new government would have among all the 13 colonies. In 1776, some of the colonies had strongly opposed any single lawmaking body that would have powers to govern all the colonies. There were a few wise delegates, however, who recognized that without a single government making laws, the individual states would be unable to work together for a common good. After more than a year of debate, the Continental Congress was ready to vote on a proposal on November 15, 1777. The compromise Articles of Confederation was then delivered to all the colonies for approval. (They would not be fully in effect until March 1781.) Even though they were a weak set of rules for governing, the articles emphasized the principle of "perpetual union," the same concept that later guided the writing of the Constitution in 1787.

By late November 1777, most of the delegates to the Continental Congress had completed their work on the Articles of Confederation and were able to return to their homes. General Washington, though, was facing his second winter as commander in chief in the field with his troops. For the second time, he was short of men, supplies, and support. With no place already prepared to accommodate his weary men, Washington was forced to build a camp at a safe distance from the British troops comfortably quartered in Philadelphia.

The commander in chief settled on a strategic plot of land about 20 miles northwest of Philadelphia, guarding the main road to New England and in view of routes into Pennsylvania and New Jersey. At Valley Forge the Continental soldiers faced one of their most severe tests of the entire war. There was every imaginable misery—starvation, disease, and depression. Men quarreled, and more than 2,000 deserted. Surprisingly, many of the American Indian allies stayed, out of loyalty to Washington, and endured the same hardships as the rest of the troops. Of 11,000 men who began the encampment in November 1777, more than 2,500 died of starvation and exposure. "No meat! No meat!" was the cry. Unscrupulous businesspeople refused to sell provisions to the army for American money, called scrip. There was simply no transport available to deliver many supplies to the winter camp. Not until March 1778, when Washington appointed his determined and resourceful friend, Nathanael Greene, as quartermaster, were the troops finally rescued from the cold and starvation.

In spite of the horror of Valley Forge, the miraculous work of Baron von Steuben with the troops throughout the winter produced a surprisingly stronger Continental army by spring than it had been in the fall. The volunteer from Prussia worked tirelessly through translators to teach the raw Americans how to move in standard formation during the confusion of battle and how to thrust properly with the bayonet. Using a simple field manual he prepared for the men, von Steuben was instrumental in keeping the troops mentally prepared for battle even when they were hungry and ill.

Washington and his army survived the almost hopeless conditions of Valley Forge and began the spring of 1778 determined to keep the British locked up in Philadelphia. In fact, the bitter winter of 1777–78 marked the end of British successes in the north. If Howe had only pressed in on Washington's troops early in the winter, he probably would have destroyed the Continental army. Leaders in Parliament finally lost patience with Howe's caution and replaced him with General Henry Clinton.

On a mild spring day early in May 1778, the hard-pressed Americans at Valley Forge rejoiced at the news that France had finally joined open alliance with the United States against the British. Fearing

Baron von Steuben trains the troops at Valley Forge as General Washington looks on, winter 1777–78. *(National Archives, Still Pictures Branch, NWDNS-111-SC-83897)*

possible attack by the French fleet, Parliament ordered the new British commander to evacuate Philadelphia and move all the British troops and equipment back to Manhattan.

Clinton realized that it would be important to keep the Americans from discovering that he was moving his troops back to New York City,

but Washington learned of the plan by June 1, 1778. Washington chose to pursue the withdrawing British cautiously and at a distance as the redcoats became stretched out along the road from Philadelphia to New York. Finally, on June 28, Washington chose to commit his main force of 5,000 men, led by Gen. Charles Lee and General Lafayette. The two forces engaged near Monmouth, New Jersey, and, largely due to the failure of Charles Lee to attack as planned, the British soon gained the upper hand. Only when Washington rode up and urged the retreating Americans to make a stand was Monmouth saved from becoming a total rout. As it was, although the Americans suffered lighter casualties (72 dead, 161 wounded, 132 missing) than the British (some 250 dead—60 of them from sunstroke—1,200 wounded, and 600 deserters), the British did manage to get the bulk of their force back to New York City, so in that sense the Americans failed to achieve their goal. In any case, the Battle of Monmouth was the last direct confrontation in the north between the main bodies of His Majesty's forces and the Continental army.

Through two years of daring maneuvers and extreme hardship, George Washington rescued the War for Independence from certain defeat. Washington's strength of character repeatedly turned retreats into stands of strength, the worst of conditions into advantages. Lafayette witnessed this strength during the Battle of Monmouth and wrote how his commander's "presence stopped the retreat." Lafayette went on to express what many Americans then and later would feel: Washington carried with him "the air best calculated to incite enthusiasm. I thought then, as now, that never had I beheld so superb a man." The colonists may not have been winning many battles in the field, but they were slowly wearing down the British by sheer doggedness. And if that doggedness had a core of idealism and a spark of inspiration, it owed much of that to George Washington.

8

FIRE AND BLOOD ACROSS THE FRONTIER

While Washington was patiently rebuilding his army at Morristown in the early summer of 1777, the American Northern Army was alert. It was faced with an aggressive invasion by the British pressing down from Canada to the interior of New York. Gen. John Burgoyne, hoping to end the war within one year, left his base above Lake Champlain in June 1777 with nearly 8,000 British, German, and Canadian troops and Indian allies. His plan to strike from the north through the "back door" of Lake Champlain into the New England colonies was the very tactic the Americans had feared back in 1775 when Benedict Arnold and Ethan Allen were sent to capture Fort Ticonderoga. This grand idea, however, became a great disaster as British arrogance and ignorance were met by Patriot cleverness and bravery.

"Gentleman Johnny" Burgoyne marched out of Fort St. Johns in northern New York in June 1777 with dozens of heavy cannon on carriages plus 30 wagon loads of officers' personal baggage, needed to maintain their camp in style. The cannon were in response to continuing British fear of American entrenchment after the fight at Breed's Hill. By July 1777, Burgoyne was successful in forcing the Americans to abandon crumbling Fort Ticonderoga by overwhelming the fort with his large artillery carefully placed on a height overlooking the fort. In spite of this return of the control of Lake Champlain to the British, the

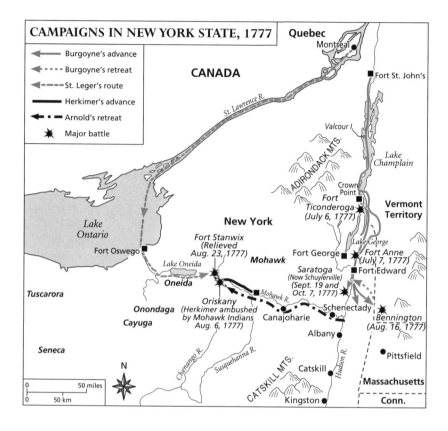

CAMPAIGNS IN NEW YORK STATE, 1777

Burgoyne's advance
Burgoyne's retreat
St. Leger's route
Herkimer's advance
Arnold's retreat
Major battle

colonial troops found it was easy to throw obstacles in his way. The Northern Army simply chopped down trees all across Burgoyne's route, sometimes slowing his progress to a mile a day. Whenever British and German troops wandered off in search of food and supplies, angry villagers met them with guns in hand. In European wars, the people in the countryside had simply hoped to avoid contact with plundering armies on the march. The colonial response was not at all what "Gentleman Johnny" had expected.

British colonel St. Leger, meanwhile, had left Montreal and turned west toward Lake Ontario to gather a smaller force of Loyalist troops and Indians from the Six Nations of the Iroquois. From there, they turned back eastward along the Mohawk Valley in order to join Burgoyne's troops at Albany, where the Mohawk and Hudson Rivers joined. In August 1777, however, St. Leger's movements stopped far short of

Albany at the American Fort Stanwix on the Mohawk River near the present town of Herkimer, New York. He was surprised by the fierce defense of the fort by Patriots under Gen. Nicholas Herkimer, a prosperous Mohawk Valley farmer, and Benedict Arnold. General Burgoyne had boasted, "I have but to give stretch to the Indian forces under my direction, and they amount to thousands, to overtake the hardened enemies of Great Britain." As early as 1710, Iroquois chiefs had visited Queen Anne and pledged their support to England during the French and Indian Wars. True to Burgoyne's claim, Mohawks under their famous chief, Joseph Brant, ambushed and nearly destroyed the reinforcements to Fort Stanwix led by General Herkimer. Nevertheless, Benedict Arnold managed to trick the Indians into believing that a huge, well-armed military force was advancing on them. More than 800 Indians quit the campaign, forcing the British to abandon their attack on the fort. St. Leger, then, was unable to complete his part of Burgoyne's three-pronged plan.

Mohawk chief Joseph Brant (1742–1807)
(National Archives, Still Pictures Branch, NWDNS-111-SC-92608)

Meanwhile, General Howe, during a hard-fought September, was convinced he could end the war by seizing the American capital of Philadelphia, so he would not be joining Burgoyne at Albany either. The scheme to isolate New England had truly fallen apart.

And General Burgoyne? Unaware of these developments, he slowly moved his ponderous baggage and troop caravan down the Hudson River Valley, dangerously far from supplies and reinforcements in Canada. By August 1777, facing shortages of food and supplies, Burgoyne sent 700 soldiers and Indian allies off into strongly Patriot territory. They headed for Bennington, Vermont, to capture American military supplies stored there. Just as at Breed's Hill, thousands of Patriot militiamen rallied, surprising the British with their strength.

New Hampshire's Col. John Stark, a hero at the Battle of Breed's Hill, attacked the approaching British forces, most of whom were German mercenaries, and killed or captured nearly all of them. (The British and German troops, including reinforcements, came to about 1,400; they lost 207 dead and 700 prisoners, plus several hundred wounded. The Americans, including reinforcements, came to about 1,850; they lost about 14 dead, while some 42 were wounded.)

The Battle of Bennington of August 16, 1777, was a long-awaited triumph for the Americans, proving once again the ability of the colonists to stand up to British and Hessian regular soldiers. It was celebrated in song and story long after the American Revolution ended. Burgoyne wrote grimly after the defeat,

> The Hampshire Grants [the Vermont territory] . . . a country unpeopled and almost unknown in the last war, now abounds in the most active and rebellious race on the continent, and hangs like a gathering storm upon my left.

During the summer of 1777, the Continental Congress had been at a loss as to who should lead the Northern Army. General Washington had appointed Gen. Philip Schuyler, but the rural New Englanders distrusted the aristocratic commander and refused to serve under him. A logical second choice was Benedict Arnold. The colonial soldiers would have followed him anywhere, but he was not in line for promotion. So early in August, the congress finally settled on Gen. Horatio Gates, a veteran of the French and Indian Wars but lacking the striking leadership qualities of Arnold.

Following the Battle of Bennington in August 1777, Vermonters flocked to strengthen the Northern Army gathering north of Albany to confront the British. It was Benedict Arnold, however, who saved this well-reinforced Patriot army from disgrace at the hands of Burgoyne. The American army was now double the size of Burgoyne's, which was his last prong standing from his original three-pronged plan. Even then the colonists' entrenched position on Bemis Heights, south of Saratoga, New York, was almost overrun by the British due to Gates's stubborn inflexibility. In September 1777, Arnold finally persuaded Gates to let him attack the British with a force of New Englanders strengthened by the superb rifle brigade of Daniel Morgan. Arnold forced the British regulars to fight, not in the open fields but in the woods, where his hit-and-run tactics were more effective. This battle at Freeman's Farm handed General Burgoyne another serious defeat and the loss of 600 more men. General Gates resented Arnold's claim to the victory, and in a petty act, he removed Arnold, a favorite of the soldiers, from his command. Near Freeman's Farm three weeks later, during a desperate attack by the British on the Americans, Arnold ignored Gates's dismissal, rushed into the battle and led a fierce assault that forced the British to pull back. This series of events also added to the dramatically unfolding puzzle of Benedict Arnold's destiny in the American Revolution.

In September 1777, just after Arnold's first bold attack on his troops at Freeman's Farm, Burgoyne received the devastating news that General Howe was in Philadelphia, not working his way up the Hudson River to join him at Albany. Now, after this second defeat, Burgoyne retreated to Saratoga, just north of Albany on the Hudson River, on October 8, 1777. There he would make his last attempt to turn the tide in his direction. Knowing Burgoyne was vulnerable, Johnny Stark and his Vermont militia managed to swing behind the British troops and cut off all hope of escape. Isolated in hostile country, without food and supplies and unable to outwit the colonists' much larger Northern Army, General Burgoyne requested terms for surrender.

At the surrender ceremony on October 17, 1777, the defeated British soldiers formally laid down their arms in neat clusters, then passed by the two generals in review. They then paraded past the assembled silent American troops. Elegantly uniformed British and Hessian regulars contrasted with the ragtag appearance of the Northern Army. The colonial army included both old men and very young boys, dressed in a variety of uniforms, and unusual battalions, such as

REVOLUTIONARY WAR

Colonel Greene's all-black Rhode Island unit. No one was prepared for this dramatic contrast between the new victor and the vanquished.

The surrender of General Burgoyne's entire army on October 17, 1777, was a catastrophe for the British and one of the great turning points of the war for independence. Unlike George Washington, whose army had scrambled and scraped its way from defeat after defeat by the British but remained intact, Burgoyne lost everything to the Americans. Surrender terms for the seven generals, 300 officers, and 5,000 soldiers captured at Saratoga included this provision: They would be safely shipped out of Boston back to England provided they pledged to never serve again in the war against the Americans. After a terrible two years of fruitless fighting and retreats, this was a stunning victory for the infant United States.

The response to Burgoyne's surrender was one of shock in Great Britain and elation in France. In London, Lord North began frantically preparing an appeal to the colonies that would settle old scores and still manage to keep the colonies under the British flag. North's Conciliatory Proposals might have been accepted by the Second Continental Congress only months before, when the colonial situation appeared grim and

The surrender of General Burgoyne at Saratoga, October 17, 1777
(National Archives)

hopeless. Arriving amidst the celebration of the great victory at Saratoga, however, North's proposals could hardly receive respectful attention. The French were finally offering open recognition and aid to the United States, and so the Americans simply dismissed North's proposals.

Since 1776, there had been vigorous and often secret efforts by Silas Deane, Benjamin Franklin, and others to persuade France to aid the colonies. Franklin was actually a great celebrity in Paris, entertained at every turn. The "simple American philosopher" dressed in Quaker gray appealed to the French ideal of the wise and witty man. After the surrender of the British at Saratoga, the French finally saw the American army as a respectable fighting force, capable of turning defeat into victory. They no longer feared joining a losing cause, perhaps finding themselves stranded in the end, confronting their old British enemy—alone. The treaty of alliance with France in February 1778 not only opened the channels for money and supplies to begin flowing to America, it also gave the support of the valuable French navy. French aid, however, did not ensure a quick, overall American victory and end to the war. While the French fleet was making its way to the American coast and supplies were beginning to leak through the British blockade, the colonial struggle continued in the remote western limits of the British colonies.

Native American resistance to white settlements away from the coastal colonies affected both American and British strategy throughout the war. Just as in the French and Indian Wars, the two sides of the conflict tried to use Native Americans to add to their troop strength. Underlying this action was the constant hope of the Indian tribes that the war efforts would end forever the movement of white settlers into their traditional lands. When the French and Indian Wars ended in 1763, the British government had attempted to keep colonial settlers out of the lands west of the Appalachian Mountains, but they were unsuccessful. By 1775, Kentucky had its first permanent white settler, not just a wandering trapper or trader like those who had roamed the frontier for years. There was a general increase in the scope and intensity of Indian attacks on white settlers during the Revolutionary War as part of this wider conflict. Most tribes joined forces with the British, but some tribes, including the Oneida, Stockbridge, and Potawatomi Indians, supported the American colonists.

The Mohawk Valley of New York became burnt-over ground as the Mohawks under Chief Joseph Brant ravaged the valley. In 1778, British

Spilling over the Mountains
FRONTIER EXPANSION AFTER 1763

WHEN THE FRENCH AND INDIAN WAR ENDED WITH A resounding British victory, virtually all of New France became English territory. That included all of Canada (except two small islands off Newfoundland) and most of the land west of the Appalachian Mountains, to the Mississippi River. The peace treaty included strong language to reserve all land west of the mountains for Native Americans. A boundary line through the mountains was declared the Proclamation Line, past which no non-Indian settlements were allowed. This was completely unenforceable. American farmers were hungry for land beyond the crowded eastern coastline, and without the French threat, they felt it was now their right to move west. Only five years after the Proclamation Line was established in 1763, treaties with the Iroquois, Cherokee, and Creek nations pushed the line further west.

Until the American Revolution, Native peoples west of the Appalachians dealt primarily with trappers, traders, and French voyageurs. Few people owned tracts of land west of the mountains, and if they did, it was wild and undeveloped. Grants were given by the Crown to French and Indian War veterans in the disputed territory, and prominent Americans such as George Washington and Benjamin Franklin hoped to secure tracts of western land for themselves.

Kentucky was a prime goal for new settlement. Expansion began immediately after the French and Indian War, with settlers flooding through such mountain passes as the Cumberland Gap and over Daniel Boone's Wilderness Road. Reports of vast hardwood forests, excellent rivers, a mild climate, and plenty of game were irresistible. By 1783, about 25,000 white settlers had moved across the mountains. As these large numbers of new settlers cultivated fields and built permanent settlements, Indian tribes recognized this as an enormous threat to their reserved land and way of life. The struggle to stop this development would go on for another century.

and Indian raids reached deep into the Wyoming Valley of north-central Pennsylvania, and the combined forces swept through central New York. After the savage destruction of the Cherry Valley settlement west of Albany, all the Patriot survivors of the battle were slaughtered. George Washington then ordered a punishing campaign against four of the Six Nations of the Iroquois: the Onondaga, Mohawk, Seneca, and Cayuga. The Oneida and Tuscarora remained neutral during most of the war, due to the efforts of their missionary, Samuel Kirkland, who made several trips with tribal leaders to Washington's camps. Some warriors from both tribes joined the American forces. So angered were the other Iroquois by this, that Joseph Brant led his Indians on raids against the stubborn tribes.

The campaign against the tribes supporting the British and terrorizing the colonial settlers spread flames throughout central New York. Many of the Iroquois lived in orderly towns of well-built houses "large and neatly finish'd . . . good log houses with stone chimneys and glass windows." As the four Iroquois tribes retreated toward Niagara and British protection, every native town and its rich fields ready for harvest were destroyed by the Americans. The effect was only to increase Indian anger and desperation, and the Iroquois remnant would continue their raids along the Mohawk Valley through 1780 and 1781. After the Revolutionary War ended, the struggle between the European settlers and the Native Americans would continue, for the tribes had signed no treaties with the new American nation.

Out in the Ohio River Valley, Native Americans aided the British in holding the vast Northwest Territory. George Rogers Clark, a 26-year-old surveyor, proposed to Governor Patrick Henry of Virginia a campaign to secure the forts and main settlements in the Ohio and Mississippi river valleys for the American cause. With fewer than 200 men, Clark set off for the wilderness interior in June 1778, sailing to the end of the Ohio River where it joined with the great Mississippi. Once there, he and his men continued west on foot. The Old Northwest Territory had a sprinkling of French settlers and a scattering of British forts in key locations. The forts, especially Detroit to the north, managed to keep the Native American tribes supplied with arms for their terrifying raids all through the region. In this way, the British kept control of the frontier lands. Clark's goal was to seize the forts, win over the French settlers to the American cause, and perhaps even establish contact with sympathetic Spaniards along the Mississippi River.

One by one the territorial outposts fell with surprising ease—Kaskaskia, Cahokia, and Prairie du Rocher on the Mississippi River, and Vincennes on the Wabash River, guarded by Fort Sackville. Worried that matters seemed to be going too smoothly, Clark determined to protect his position by arranging a crucial truce with chiefs of the area's enemy tribes. Detroit, however, remained British. Lt. Col. Henry Hamilton (called "Hair Buyer" because he paid Indians for scalps they brought in) prepared to recover the stolen forts for the British. With a small force, he marched the hundreds of miles from Detroit on Lake Erie to Vincennes in the Ohio Valley and seized Vincennes from Clark's occupiers without a shot. As December floodwaters covered much of the lowlands, Vincennes appeared securely in British hands.

Based at Kaskaskia, Clark was fortunately resupplied by shipments up the Mississippi River from Oliver Pollack, an American merchant in New Orleans. Despite the floodwaters, Clark decided to move immediately against Hamilton at Vincennes. Leading his group of "Long Knives" through deep, icy water for much of the 18-day journey, Clark reached the fortress on the Wabash River. One of Clark's men later wrote: "Having no other resource but wading this . . . lake of water, we plunged into it with courage, Colonel Clark being first." Short of ammunition and food, weakened from the nightmarish march, Clark's men viewed the strong fort's palisade walls and drew back. Clark, however, gambled that Hamilton could be tricked into defeat. Hamilton had strengthened his position in the fort with additional Native American reinforcements. Clark managed to deceive the fort's inhabitants into thinking he had arrived in great strength. Rumors of a large, well-armed American force influenced most of Hamilton's Indian supporters to abandon him, and in another surprising turn of events, Clark recovered the fort and Vincennes with little effort. The February 23, 1779, "Night

Fort Sackville, Indiana, 1779 *(National Archives)*

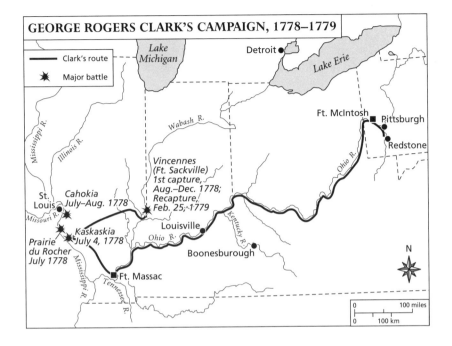

GEORGE ROGERS CLARK'S CAMPAIGN, 1778–1779

Clark's route

Major battle

Lake Michigan

Detroit

Lake Erie

Ft. McIntosh

Pittsburgh

Redstone

Mississippi R.

Illinois R.

Wabash R.

Ohio R.

Vincennes
(Ft. Sackville)
1st capture,
Aug.–Dec. 1778;
Recapture,
Feb. 25, 1779

St. Louis

Cahokia
July–Aug. 1778

Missouri R.

Kaskaskia
July 4, 1778

Prairie
du Rocher
July 1778

Mississippi R.

Tennessee R.

Ft. Massac

Louisville

Ohio R.

Kentucky R.

Boonesburough

N

0   100 miles

0   100 km

of the Long Knives" in Indiana paralleled Benedict Arnold's clever trickery at Fort Stanwix in 1777 against St. Leger's Mohawk Indian allies in New York. Both had gambled by creating the illusion of a larger force preparing for attack—and both had won.

George Rogers Clark continued to hold the "Illinois Country" for the United States until the end of the war, claiming the territory for the colony of Virginia. Although Detroit remained in British hands until the end of the war, Clark's efforts paid off richly when the War for Independence ended. The Treaty of Paris would give the Kentucky territory and all of the Old Northwest Territory (Ohio, Indiana, Michigan, Illinois, Wisconsin, and part of Minnesota) to the United States. Before George Rogers Clark's conquests could have any lasting importance, however, there was still much bloody fighting to be done, and not all of it was on land.

9

MANEUVERS AT SEA

On a frosty day in February of 1776, a small squadron of warships bearing the American colors set sail from Philadelphia for Chesapeake Bay, almost 250 miles down the Delaware River and along the coast of the Atlantic Ocean. The ships were forced to break a coating of ice in the same channel that Washington would cross in his famous attack on Trenton in December of that very year. Compared to the Royal Navy of Great Britain, this flotilla was pitiful, but it represented the beginning of the American navy. Aboard the flagship, the *Alfred,* and in command of this new navy was Esek Hopkins, a veteran commercial seaman appointed admiral by the Naval Committee for the colonies.

As early as the fall of 1775, George Washington recognized the need for an American navy. If there had been American ships to face the British fleet in Boston Harbor, the task of driving the redcoats out of Boston after the Battle of Breed's Hill might not have taken so long. The construction of a fighting ship, however, required months, not to mention enormous amounts of material, engineering skill and just plain money.

The American coastal colonies had a shipbuilding industry at the beginning of the war, but the demand for ships at that time was limited to commercial and fishing vessels. There were no American naval architects with the experience necessary to design anything like the great British warships. The colonies did have plenty of timber for ship construction, however. During the early years of settlement, in the vast forests of the northern colonies in particular, farmers and woodsmen marked the tallest and sturdiest pine trees in the woods for ships' masts. These "King's trees" would be carted off to England to make English ships. None of the shipyards in such cities as Boston, Portsmouth, New

York, and Charleston had the shipwrights or equipment needed to assemble anything that could sail as fast or carry as many guns as the British battleships. Furthermore, the colonies had no foundries capable of forging the big guns to arm warships.

Any decision to establish a national navy rested with the Continental Congress. At the meeting of the Second Continental Congress in the fall of 1775, members recognized that the colonies could not expect to be a threat to the British navy in any kind of direct conflict. It might be possible, though, for smaller, more maneuverable ships the size of frigates (used like the modern cruiser or destroyer) to interrupt shipments of supplies up and down the coast of the colonies. Washington himself used such a strategy during the siege of Boston. Even before the formation of an American navy, the new commander in chief arranged for the assembly of a small fleet of American ships to capture ammunition and other supplies bound for Boston to help the redcoats and the Loyalists. Washington's plan worked. During the winter of 1775–76, the Americans used converted fishing boats and small merchant ships to capture 35 British cargo vessels. As a result, tons of valuable war goods made their way into the hands of needy Patriots surrounding the city.

Esek Hopkins
(1718–1802)
(National Archives,
Still Pictures Branch,
NWDNS-148-GW-461)

"For the protection and defense of the United Colonies," the delegates of the Continental Congress approved the refitting of 13 merchant ships as naval frigates in the autumn of 1775. By the spring of the following year, the Continental navy had Esek Hopkins of Rhode Island as its first commander. A merchant seaman for 40 years, Hopkins was pleased to lead the new navy but called the Naval Committee "a pack of damn fools" for assuming that a national navy could help finance the war by seizing the cargo of enemy ships.

In the late winter of 1776, Hopkins received his first assignment: Take a small fleet into Chesapeake Bay and hunt British ships. Commodore Hopkins, however, did not linger in Chesapeake Bay. Instead he saw a more important opportunity and directed his ships to the islands of the Bahamas, southeast of Florida, where he could capture gunpowder, ammunition, and other war supplies from the islands' British royal governor, supplies that Washington's army desperately needed. Hopkins's plan was successful, and he returned with a prize of 88 cannon, other heavy guns, and two dozen barrels of gunpowder. This was the first profitable mission undertaken by the Continental navy.

Esek Hopkins's flagship, the *Alfred,* carried the new Continental flag—and a 29-year-old first lieutenant, John Paul Jones. The original flag of the united colonies was called the Grand Union and was stitched in Philadelphia by Margaret Manny, a seamstress. Manny designed the flag with 13 red and white stripes. In the upper left corner was a blue square with the crosses of St. Andrew and St. George (representing the union of England and Scotland), not the 13 stars, which came later, in June 1777. The flag flew from the mast to identify its ship as American, not just a ship from one of the separate colonies. It was a flag of this design that received the first recognition from a foreign country, as Hopkins and his fleet sailed into the harbor of the Dutch island St. Eustatius in the West Indies on November 16, 1776.

Altogether there were 53 ships that actively served in the Continental navy during the entire war. Thirteen of these were frigates, medium-size ships with 28 to 44 guns. The remaining ships were the size of sloops or schooners, both of which were the type used before and during the war for fishing and carrying freight up and down the coast. The Continental navy did not have any ships of the line (the term for the most powerful ships available), the kind that carried at least 64 guns, while the British boasted 72 ships of the line. The smaller craft like the sloop, however, with a dozen or so small cannon mounted below deck and a few small-caliber deck guns, were better suited to the kind of sea warfare the Americans fought. The smaller ships were much faster and more maneuverable than the heavy ships of the line. The common method of sea fighting at the time of the revolution was for ships to line up side by side within range of their cannon and fire broadsides at each other. A ship of the line could fire as much as 60 tons of cannon shot in a single volley. These enormous vessels were, however, unable to change position quickly, a serious disadvantage when fighting at close range with smaller craft like the American sloops.

Having relatively small ships was not the only problem that faced the Continental navy. The colonies had trouble working together to create a national navy. Instead of cooperating to finance the construction of a single fleet, individual colonies commissioned their own ships. Often these ships and their crews tried to protect their own colonial commercial interests without any support from the neighboring colonies. A typical use of a "state navy" would be to escort merchant ships through dangerous waters where there was a threat of British seizure. These dangerous waters were not always the Atlantic. Frequently they were rivers, inlets, and bays, such as Chesapeake Bay. Any one of these vital waterways could have enemy warships lurking to ambush American ships loaded with cargo to be traded either in European ports or, more likely, the Caribbean islands.

The state navies accomplished little for themselves or for the common good of the Revolution. Too often they were made up of converted cargo ships without enough heavy guns to match those of the British frigates and brigs (light, two-masted craft). Furthermore, the sailors responsible for operating the state fleets were inexperienced and clumsy by European standards.

Many merchants were still nervous about moving their ships from American ports. Merchants of Philadelphia, for example, were not able to rely on the protection of either their own state navy or a national fleet during the final months of the war. To provide more security for their trade ships, they armed their own ship, the *Hyder Ally,* commanded by Capt. Joshua Barney. The *Hyder Ally* was fitted with only 16 guns, yet it was expected to defend the Philadelphia trade ships against enemy warships, which were much better armed and had more experienced crews.

One of the most humiliating battles between a state navy and the British occurred in the summer of 1779. The Massachusetts navy, with 19 lightly armed ships, escorted approximately 20 additional vessels carrying militia headed for Penobscot Bay in Maine. Their objective was to capture a store of supplies protected there by many of the Loyalists who had left Boston after the siege of the city in the spring of 1776.

The Massachusetts expedition was unable to capture the fortress at Penobscot Bay, however, because of faulty coordination and poor judgment by the commanders. While the assault forces from Massachusetts were trying to persuade the Tories manning the fort to surrender, a 64-gun royal ship of the line and a squadron of smaller British warships arrived at the mouth of the bay. Commanders of the Massachusetts fleet tried to escape by sailing up the Penobscot River, but their flight was doomed. Eventually they abandoned their ships and set them afire to prevent capture and later use by the British. This enormous loss was a major setback for Massachusetts and its continuing contribution to the war effort. Other state navies had similar disastrous experiences and had little, if any, impact on the royal fleet, which moved wherever and whenever it chose before France entered the war. One exception was Connecticut, which used its fleet to serve in the defense of the country. The ships sponsored by Connecticut sailed back and forth between the colony and the islands of the West Indies, bringing back the vital sulfur necessary for making gunpowder.

The determination of each colony to maintain its own navy was not the only reason that a national navy was slow in getting started. More often than not, the best fighting ships in any colonial port were privately owned and manned by crews who hired on for their own profit. They were not interested in serving a colony and least of all in serving a country. The owners and commanders of these ships were called privateers, and they did more damage to the British than the combined state navies and the Continental navy. Privateering was far more appealing to a seaman than serving aboard a naval vessel. A job as a crewman aboard a privateer required less discipline aboard the ship and promised a better wage at the end of a raid, since crewmen were rewarded with part of the profits from any booty captured. The new Continental navy was unable to attract many volunteers for service because of low wages and miserable conditions. As a result, most of the men who sailed in the American navy were not sailors by choice. They were assigned or ordered to serve as seamen rather than infantrymen.

Privateering, or commerce raiding, was not only approved by individual states but was often the only reason for many states to have their own fleets. The scheme was simple enough. A state would arrange a

Learning the Ropes
COMMANDING THE NAVY

WHEN THE AMERICAN REVOLUTION BEGAN, THE colonies had neither warships nor sailors trained to man them. The colonies never lacked for volunteers for their tiny new navy, but these men were not prepared to operate a warship. A merchant ship or fishing boat outfitted for war was useless if the crew aboard it was not trained. Crewmen needed to act as a single fighting unit when the ship was engaged in battle. The only way to avoid chaos was for every man aboard the ship to have an assigned duty. Gunners who loaded, fired, and then swabbed the muzzle of a ship's cannon had to work without thinking. In the frenzy of attack, trained and clear-thinking commanders were essential.

The young colonial navy never had enough commanders or junior officers to face the huge and experienced British navy. When a man volunteered for service in the new American navy, he entered as an ordinary sailor. A few select men qualified for officer rank. Since there were no officers' schools to teach officer candidates, midshipmen had to prove themselves in actual fighting conditions.

The American navy remained in a state of development until the end of the war because the cost of building ships and training sailors and officers was too expensive. Consequently, most of the important sea engagements between the Americans and the British were carried out by privateers such as John Paul Jones. Privateering crews were not burdened by the rigid discipline the navy demanded. In all, only 53 ships sailed as American naval vessels during the war, and most were relatively small. It remained for the French fleet to provide the seapower that the Americans needed to defeat the British at Yorktown and end the war.

contract with a private shipowner to attack and capture cargo or supply ships belonging to the British. Often, the state's only expense was to fit or arm the ship and to provide some sort of insurance to guarantee that the owner of the ship would not lose in the venture. The net gain for the states could mean thousands of dollars' worth (by today's standards) of war supplies such as weapons, ammunition, gunpowder, and cloth for tents and uniforms. If the cargo seized was not war supplies, then the cash from the sale of the freight would go into the treasury of

REVOLUTIONARY WAR

John Paul Jones
(1747–1792)
(National Archives)

the state. A percentage of that profit would be divided among the ship's commander and his crew.

Eventually this scheme might benefit the Continental army and the cause of the Revolution, since the arms or cash would go to support the war. Unfortunately, however, there were too many privateers whose only interest was to make a killing on the profit from their raids. They would sell whatever they had captured in European ports—Dutch, French, and even British—for the highest price they could get. The American market could not compete in any kind of bidding war with European merchants because the American treasury was broke. Unless the American bidder could offer a payment in hard cash (silver), he had little chance of competing in a world market. American currency was next to worthless.

The best-known and perhaps the most glamorous of American Revolution naval heroes was John Paul Jones. A Scotsman by birth, his name was actually John Paul, and from the age of 12 he went to sea on British ships. He added the name of Jones to change his identity when he fled to America in 1773 after he had been accused of two murders during his service in the British merchant fleet. When the Revolution broke out, he went to Philadelphia and in December 1775 gained a commission with the new navy, joining the *Alfred* as first lieutenant. Promoted to captain and given command of the *Providence* in 1776, on one voyage alone he captured 16 ships for the American cause. Soon recognized by the colonial government as well as by the British as a man of extraordinary skill, daring, and courage, Jones had decided to fight for the colonists because of his belief in the rights of common people. He refused, however, to declare himself an American, but instead called himself a citizen of the world, or as he wrote: "Tho' I have drawn my sword in the present generous struggle for the rights of men . . . I am not in arms as an American."

His most important mission came when he was given the command of the *Ranger* in 1778 and ordered to France; operating out of French ports, he was assigned to deliver the same kind of destructive force on British coastal towns and cities that the British had ruthlessly dealt to American cities. Benjamin Franklin and the Continental Congress had devised a plan to have American raiding parties secretly enter English cities such as Liverpool and even London and set them afire. No one else in the colonies seemed quite as capable of carrying this out as John Paul Jones. A plan to sabotage London and the Royal Palace was never executed, but he did lead raids on English shipping and ports, including one on Whitehaven, a port on the Irish Sea. His objective was to capture and burn the city as well as ships in the harbor; the plan failed because one of his crew was a traitor and warned the people in the town.

Determined not to be defeated by this failure, a few days later Jones launched his most daring raid. He slipped ashore in Scotland with the intention of kidnapping an Englishman of noble rank and then exchanging him for American prisoners held by the British. The nobleman was not home, but Jones and his crew stole the family's silver tableware and serving pieces. To prevent having his intentions misunderstood, Jones returned them to the family with the explanation that his motive was not the "pursuit of riches."

Typical of his courage was Jones's famous fight in the North Atlantic Sea off the coast of Scotland. In a converted freighter donated by the French, armed with 40 less-than-trustworthy guns, Jones was cruising around the British Isles in the late summer of 1779. Jones had named his ship *Bonhomme Richard* after Benjamin Franklin's *Poor Richard's Almanac*. His purpose was to disrupt British shipping; he was not reluctant to attack anything sailing under the English flag. The *Bonhomme Richard* and its small accompanying flotilla of little boats found a target on September 23, 1779. A convoy of British ships escorted by the *Serapis,* a 50-gun warship, came into view.

For hours the *Serapis* and *Bonhomme Richard* fired broadsides at each other. Eventually Jones lashed his ship to the *Serapis,* and their crews fought hand to hand with pistols and cutlasses. There is a famous story of Jones's response to the threats from the *Serapis*'s commander. When ordered to give up, Jones replied, "I have not yet begun to fight." Whether or not these were the exact words, Jones and the *Bonhomme Richard* forced the British ship to strike, or surrender, with its mainmast

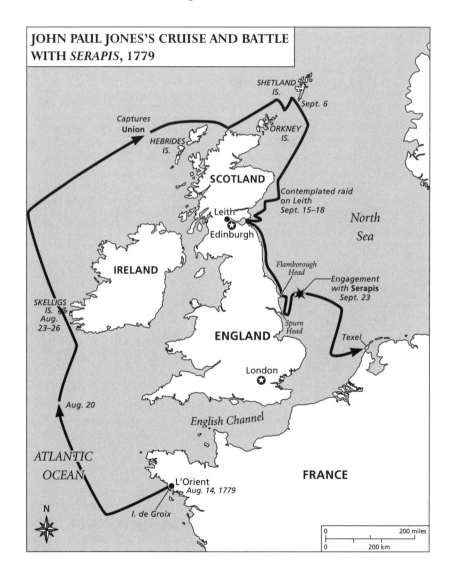

JOHN PAUL JONES'S CRUISE AND BATTLE WITH *SERAPIS*, 1779

John Paul Jones
leads the capture
of the *Serapis*.
(National Archives)

shot to splinters and the crew unable to continue fighting. A short time
later, Jones and his crew boarded the captured *Serapis* and watched as
the *Richard* sank.

The history of the U.S. Navy, and in fact the history of all naval battles, can claim few stories of more savage fighting than that of the *Bonhomme Richard* and the *Serapis*. The British captain declared later in
testimony that the American ship was driven by a determination "of a
most unalterable resolution." The status of John Paul Jones as revolutionary hero today seems quite inconsistent with the sad conclusion to
his life. After the war, he became an adviser to the Russian Crown for
the purpose of building a navy. Not many years later, he died penniless
and unknown in Paris. (In 1913, his remains were brought to the U.S.
Naval Academy in Annapolis, where today they lie in a crypt.)

Prospects for a navy strong enough to threaten the British remained
dim throughout the war. During the first half of the war, the Royal Navy
was generally able to move at will with little resistance. Fortunately for
the American cause, the British were finally challenged in the struggle

to control the seas by the alliance with France signed in the spring of 1778. With the entrance of France into the war, the Americans hoped that the British command of the seas would be broken.

The French navy had undergone a period of rebuilding since the end of the French and Indian Wars. By the beginning of the American war for independence, France was able to dispatch a fleet at least as strong as that of the British navy. Furthermore, many of the French ships were new or refitted to meet the standards of some of the world's best naval engineers. French officers and sailors were highly disciplined and ready for battle. A strong ally of France at the start of the revolution was Spain, and the combined navies of France and Spain added up to more ships than the British navy had. Between them, France and Spain had 90 ships of the line to compare to Britain's 72. The Spanish ships were much inferior to the faster and better-manned French, but the two navies together presented a sobering threat to the British naval supremacy that the colonies had faced during the first two and a half years of the war.

Other developments in Europe soon increased the threat to the British navy. In addition to French naval assistance, the American cause benefited from a coalition of other sympathetic European nations. Russia, Sweden, Denmark, Prussia, Portugal, and the Kingdom of Naples (then an independent state in Italy) joined together in an alliance in 1779 called the League of Armed Neutrality. They agreed to disrupt British war traffic on the seas, since they had all been the victims of British attacks on neutral shipping and could not resist an opportunity to get even. The addition of these other European navies suddenly shifted the balance in the American Revolution. What had begun as a struggle between a single world power and some of its rebellious colonies had become a world conflict.

While France was rebuilding its fleet, the Royal Navy of Great Britain was in decline. Living and working conditions in the navy were so bad that in the years between 1774 and 1780, 60,000 British sailors died from sickness or deserted. There was such a serious shortage of sailors that the government approved impressment, or kidnapping of able-bodied men from other jobs or ships, forcing them to serve in the navy. Yet the minister of the Royal Navy, the earl of Sandwich, stated that he had neither interest nor time to talk about the problem. Even new ships being built were put together with poor workmanship and materials. For the first time in many years, conditions were so bad that England feared the French naval threat.

To the disappointment of George Washington and the entire American resistance, the alliance with France was not as helpful in the beginning as they had hoped. The first opportunity for the French fleet to come to the aid of the Americans was in the spring of 1778. Gen. Henry Clinton, newly appointed commander of British forces in the colonies (replacing Gen. William Gage), decided to evacuate Philadelphia, which Washington had surrounded with his troops. Clinton's plan was to shift his troops to New York City. General Washington learned about the plan and recognized that he had a perfect opportunity to attack Clinton and defeat the main body of the British army while it tried to escape from Philadelphia to New York. Washington knew, however, that a land assault would not be enough; he would need the help of the French navy to intercept British transport ships loading troops and supplies at the mouth of the Delaware River. Washington's decision to attack the British at Monmouth, about halfway between Philadelphia and New York City, was part of the strategy to combine American land forces and the French navy to deliver a destructive blow to the British main army and perhaps end the war.

Unfortunately, the French fleet did not arrive at the Delaware River until July 8, 1778, largely because its commander, Admiral d'Estaing, took too much time crossing the Atlantic. As a result of d'Estaing's tardiness, the plan failed and the British troops were able to reach New York. When the French fleet did finally arrive, they still had an opportunity to weaken the British by attacking their warships anchored in New York Harbor. D'Estaing's fleet was much larger and better built than that of the British, but he refused to enter the harbor because he feared his ships were too heavy to cross its shallow, sandy entrance. Washington and other American commanders were enraged but reluctant to criticize the new American ally. Many more misunderstandings between the Continental army and the French navy occurred before the war's end, but eventually the combined forces of American foot soldiers and French ships were crucial in bringing victory to the rebels.

The lost opportunity to defeat General Clinton and the British in the spring of 1778 and possibly end the war (already three years long) was a bitter disappointment for General Washington and the Americans. Little did they know that the war would drag on for four more years. During that time, more disappointments would come, not only to General Washington but also to all the Americans, whose energies and resources were becoming exhausted.

10
MONEY, MUTINY, AND MORALE

What were the seven long war years like for the general population, who had to continue their planting and harvesting, their businesses, their child-rearing, and their social activities? In the first two years of the war, there was a great surge of patriotism and self-sacrifice, except among the disgruntled Loyalists, of course. All things English were self-righteously avoided, and a premium was placed on any habit, product, or style labeled American. There was a high-spirited enthusiasm for the idealism of the cause. Colonials took pride in being the underdog courageously taking on the mighty but corrupt British Empire. This unity and commitment to sacrifice broke down as colonial society began to react to the slow and disheartening war effort according to each individual's level of prosperity or group distinctions.

The war was experienced differently by the wealthy and by the poor. Throughout the war, all the major colonial cities were seized and occupied by British troops at one time or another. During those times, a high society flourished, with extravagant spending, feasting, and dancing. It was a tempting lifestyle that eventually appealed to upper-class American Patriots as well. As the earlier responses of self-sacrifice in 1776 lost their appeal, by 1778 more and more rich Patriots such as John Hancock could be found imitating the elegant and spendthrift ways of British officers. It was this lifestyle that Benedict Arnold found himself enjoying in Philadelphia after General Howe's troops departed from the city in June 1778, when they feared the arrival of the French fleet.

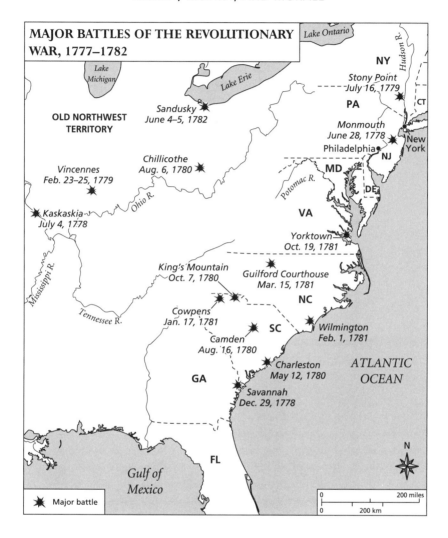

MAJOR BATTLES OF THE REVOLUTIONARY
WAR, 1777–1782

Lake Ontario

NY

Stony Point
July 16, 1779

PA

Lake Michigan

Lake Erie

CT

OLD NORTHWEST
TERRITORY

Sandusky
June 4–5, 1782

Monmouth
June 28, 1778

Philadelphia

New
York

NJ

Chillicothe
Aug. 6, 1780

Vincennes
Feb. 23–25, 1779

MD

Potomac R.

DE

Ohio R.

Kaskaskia
July 4, 1778

VA

Yorktown
Oct. 19, 1781

Mississippi R.

King's Mountain
Oct. 7, 1780

Guilford Courthouse
Mar. 15, 1781

Tennessee R.

Cowpens
Jan. 17, 1781

NC

Camden
Aug. 16, 1780

SC

Wilmington
Feb. 1, 1781

Charleston
May 12, 1780

ATLANTIC
OCEAN

GA

Savannah
Dec. 29, 1778

Hudson R.

N

FL

Gulf of
Mexico

0   200 miles

0   200 km

✸ Major battle

Not many colonial families were wealthy, however. Most people made a modest living as farmers, and women and children left behind on the farms found themselves taking on tasks they rarely had done by themselves before. By the end of 1776, fathers and sons no longer enlisted for just six months but for one to three years. Mothers and young children had to carry out all the farm work, from planting through harvest. They waited uncertainly from month to month for a father's army paycheck, but those wages were small and frequently not paid on time. The women struggled to replace worn homespun uniforms and bedding for loved ones in the army as well as their own families, but spinning and weaving by hand took a long time. With all the farm work to do, when did the women have time to make clothing?

Women and children were called upon for even stranger tasks than farm chores. For instance, a shortage of salt threatened everyone's survival. Without salt, meat could not be preserved, fisheries had to be shut down, and the Continental army could not be fed. It was said that two things were necessary to win the war: gunpowder and salt. When the British succeeded in cutting off all salt supplies to the colonies in 1777, riots occurred outside warehouses. Benjamin Franklin knew that the emergency salt shipments to the colonies from the West Indies would not be enough, so he distributed information about the production of salt from sea water. As salt works were established along the coastline, John Adams commented in 1777 that "all the old women and children are gone down to the Jersey shore to make salt."

Women did not serve just at home. "Molly Pitcher" was a generic nickname used to describe women who provided critical support to men in the field. Camping next to the battlefields, women delivered food and drink to the soldiers, sometimes in the heat of combat. They nursed the sick and wounded, mended, washed, and cooked. But they also took on dangerous missions as spies and even as soldiers themselves when their husbands fell at their posts. The best-known "Molly Pitcher" was Mary Ludwig Hays McCauley, who replaced her stricken husband at the Battle of Monmouth and rallied the troops. After the battle, she was commissioned as a sergeant by none other than General Washington himself. Deborah Sampson of Plympton, Massachusetts, on the other hand, was determined to serve as a soldier from the beginning. She enlisted in 1782 in her handmade uniform as Robert Shurtleff. In order to avoid detection, she tended her own battle wounds and bathed before sunrise. General Paterson chose her as his orderly, and it was not until she accompanied him to Philadelphia in 1783 that her identity was revealed. When she was gravely ill from a fever epidemic, Deborah Sampson's sex was discovered by her physician, and she was given an honorable discharge by General Paterson. At the end of the war, some women, including Mary McCauley and Deborah Sampson, received military pensions and medals for bravery.

The war also created great changes and uncertainties for those who did not work the land. The fishing and shipping industries were ruined

MONEY, MUTINY, AND MORALE

A copy of a J. C. Armytage engraving, *Molly Pitcher at the Battle of Monmouth,* June 1778, showing Mary McCauley (who became known as Molly Pitcher) *(National Archives/DOD War & Conflict, #0037)*

in the northern colonies by the wartime blockades of the British. Idle seamen who were not serving in the military were glad to join the privateers—the private ships authorized by the Continental Congress to capture foreign cargoes. There was a thin line between patriotic seizure and plain piracy. This line was often crossed for personal profit, and sailors on the privateers were suspect wherever they appeared.

Some Americans were affected by the war quite differently from the usual colonial citizen. From the very beginning of the war, certain groups in the colonies were determined to remain neutral as events moved more and more toward violent conflict. Several Protestant sects such as the Mennonites, Quakers, Dunkards, and Moravians opposed the use of force to settle disputes, but few of them were Loyalists. In keeping with their religious beliefs, members of these groups served on Revolutionary Committees and found many ways to aid the Patriot cause. The Moravians in North Carolina, for instance, voluntarily paid three times the taxes of other citizens and worked in many hospitals. The Dunkard community at Ephrata, Pennsylvania, turned over some of its large buildings to be used as hospitals.

Another group served in the war for unique reasons. Both the British and the colonial armies hoped to take advantage of the huge African-American population in America, primarily in the southern colonies. As early as 1775 in Virginia, the British offered freedom to any African American "able and willing to bear arms for the King's cause." Southern Patriots such as Patrick Henry became alarmed that thousands of slaves would flee into British safety and the promise of freedom.

As early as Lexington and Concord and the Battle at Breed's Hill, free black men had fought side by side with other colonial Patriots. Colonists

The Life of Venture Smith

WHEN THOMAS JEFFERSON WROTE THE LINES FOR which he is best known to most Americans—"We hold these truths to be self-evident, that all men are created equal"—he owned 150 slaves at his Virginia plantation, Monticello. Jefferson believed African slaves were intellectually inferior to white Europeans; therefore, they needed the guidance and protection of their masters. One of many slaves who proved Jefferson wrong was Venture Smith.

Venture Smith arrived in Rhode Island as a nine-year-old boy from Africa in the 1730s. He grew up to be a large, strong adult and became known as a difficult slave to manage. One day after he was married, he defended his wife in a dispute. As a result, he was sold a number of times to other masters and never allowed to reunite with his wife and small children while a slave.

Smith, however, was patient and industrious. By arranging to work as a hired man, he was able to pay his master what he owed in weekly expenses and earn enough as well to set aside for himself. By the age of 36, he had saved enough to buy his own freedom—71 English pounds sterling, the price of 4,000 acres. This was in 1765, the year of the Stamp Act.

Gradually Smith purchased freedom for his wife and four children, and then he set his goal on buying his own land. He earned money by cutting and hauling firewood for wealthy Connecticut landholders. A curious detail in Smith's story is his purchase of a slave to help him once he owned his own land. It was a poor investment, however, because the slave ran away, and Venture Smith never recovered him.

Venture Smith died as an old man in Connecticut in 1805, a successful farmer and owner of more than 100 acres and three houses.

were cheered by these contributions, but what about black men still in bondage? Should they also be encouraged to join the Patriot cause? Both General Washington and the Continental Congress were opposed to accepting African-American slaves as soldiers, but in response to the British recruitment of slaves in the fall of 1775, they changed their minds. Like Patrick Henry, they feared a great movement by slaves to the British side and finally agreed to encourage African-American slaves to support their revolutionary efforts. By 1777, a Hessian officer remarked, "One sees no [colonial] regiment in which there are not negroes in abundance, and among them are able-bodied, sturdy fellows." Some colonies, such as Rhode Island, actually purchased the freedom of slaves before accepting them as soldiers, while in other colonies, individual slaves were promised their freedom by their owners once their time of service was over. It became convenient for wealthy families to donate their black servants as soldiers in place of their own fathers and sons to fill the quotas required of each colony by the Continental Congress. However, the offer of freedom to slaves for service in the Continental army was immediately opposed by Patriot slaveholders in southern states, who feared it would cause slave uprisings and economic ruin.

Eventually, more than 750 black men served with the colonial troops. In response to the British offers of freedom and money, records suggest that many thousands of slaves in the southern colonies served the British, some of them joining the British Ethiopian regiment. Other African Americans took advantage of the conflict to escape from their masters into forests and swamps. For slaves, the Revolution held their only hope for personal freedom through escape or military service for one side or the other. Three all-black regiments fought for independence. Rarely entrusted with major roles or responsibility, black people nevertheless were valuable to the Patriots as craftspeople, construction workers, ships' pilots, and even spies.

The many Indian tribes throughout the colonies were greatly affected by the Revolutionary War. Like the black population, the Native American people in eastern North America became involved in the war for independence for different reasons from the white colonists. The Patriots feared that the addition of Indian forces would strengthen the British efforts to defeat them. On the path toward war, in 1775, the Continental Congress sought to direct Indian interests by establishing an Indian Commission. The goal was to persuade the many different tribes to remain neutral in the conflict. At the same time, Great Britain had 50

Red Jacket, a Seneca chief, was among the Native American leaders who sided with the British during the war. After the war Washington presented Red Jacket with a silver medal, shown in this engraving, as a gesture of goodwill between the Americans and the Seneca. *(Library of Congress, Print & Photographs Division [LC-USZ62-125642])*

officers dedicated to contacts with the Indians in hopes that the Indians would support their side. The colonists were well aware that certain tribes were traditional allies of the British, for example, the Six Nations of the Iroquois who had pledged their allegiance to Queen Anne in 1710. Many tribes also had much to lose by colonial success; it was the westward pressure from the coastal colonies that kept threatening tribal lands.

By the spring of 1776, it was already evident that it would be impossible to prevent active Indian involvement in the war. Encouraged by George Washington, the Continental Congress then began to approach certain tribes for support. The Indians of the upper New York territory clearly favored the British, and the tribes in the southern colonies were taking advantage of the growing instability in the southern colonies to carry out their own raids against colonial settlements. That left only the northern tribes as possible allies.

Some northern tribes had already aided colonial efforts. In 1775, 19 Abenaki joined Benedict Arnold on his march to Quebec, with such individuals as Sabatis and Eneas later serving as valued messengers. Washington hoped to get as many as 600 recruits from the St. John, Nova Scotia, Penobscot, and Passamaquoddy Indians, but these tribes proved much harder to employ. Tribal leaders saw no benefit in the war to their tribes unless they received substantial compensation in exchange for their support. In spite of a plea from the respected Ethan Allen, the Caughnawaga Mohawk felt the same. The poverty-stricken Continental Congress had little to offer, and in the end, those tribes contributed little to the war effort. Only the Stockbridge Indians of western Massachusetts were ready to join the independence effort. Eventually, aid came from Cherokee, Choctaw, and Catawba as well, both as scouts and as soldiers.

In the western territories of the Ohio River Valley, the tribes were clearly under British influence until George Rogers Clark began his mission of removing the valley forts from British control. He met with many Native Americans, using his French friends in the river valley to help persuade many of the tribes that the colonial cause was a noble one. Several of the tribal groups decided to withdraw support from the British, and in the words of the Peankeshaw chief, Turtle's Son, "to tell all the red people on the Wabash [River] to bloody the land no more for the English." While there were never large numbers of Indians allied with the colonists in the Ohio territories, Clark's efforts completely altered the traditional alliances and began a transition to American domination over the region.

Tribal life was greatly disrupted all across North America, as some tribes, such as the Oneida and Tuscarora, found themselves under attack from their own fellow Iroquois for favoring independence or neutrality, while others, such as the Ohio Valley tribes, found their traditional trade alliances changing as they began to pull back from supporting the British in response to the appeals of George Rogers Clark. The British encouraged savage raids by Indian tribes on frontier settlements, especially in the upper New York region; consequently, George Washington unleashed a massive counterattack in the Sullivan Expedition. Most of the Iroquois villages and fields were completely destroyed in this 1779 effort to eliminate the Indian threat in upstate New York. Indians who sought refuge in or near American forts had few provisions, often dying of starvation, exposure, or smallpox. Many notable individuals of several tribes aided the Revolutionary War effort and were honored by their American leaders, but most of the people in their tribes suffered by being caught in the middle of a war that was not of their own making.

George Rogers Clark persuades Indians at Cahokia to support the American rebels. *(National Archives, Still Pictures Branch, NWDNS-66-G-5-108)*

Their traditional way of life was often altered permanently, as with the Oneida, Tuscarora, and Stockbridge tribes, who were persuaded to sell all their lands to New York State after the war ended. They moved to Wisconsin in hopes of rebuilding their tribal lives.

Everyone in the colonies was affected by the shortages caused by the disruption of war. Crop harvests were lean because so few men were still home to cultivate the soil. Farms were overrun by competing armies, and homesteads were constantly raided by all sides. The trade blockade by the British navy also created shortages of imported items, so some merchants hoarded these products, selling them at huge profits. At the beginning of the war, a Patriot commented that "no one then even dreamt that our struggles against the common oppressor would involve us in mutual oppressions of each other." Profit-taking (as high

Molly Brant and the Iroquois

MOLLY BRANT WAS THE SISTER OF JOSEPH BRANT, A powerful leader of Iroquois warriors allied with the English during the American Revolution. The Brants were Mohawk, one of the tribes that formed the Iroquois confederation, and women have strong roles in Mohawk culture. Molly Brant's position was doubly strengthened by her being the widow of British Indian agent Sir William Johnson. Once the American Revolution began, she was pivotal in persuading the Iroquois to stand fast with the British.

This imagined portrait of Molly Brant depicts her as Mohawk, Loyalist, and Euro-Canadian. *(Canada Post Corporation, 1986. Reproduced with permission. National Archives of Canada/POS4285)*

Brant served the Iroquois as, in the words of British colonel Daniel Claus, "their Confidant in every Matter of Importance . . . and prevented many a mischief." During the war, Molly Brant fled to Fort Niagara, where she lived in a house built for her by the British. There she urged the Indian warriors to remain loyal to the king of England and to fight on. She was so valuable that a British officer, Gen. Frederick Haldimand, commander of British forces in Canada, instructed "that Miss Molly is to act as she thinks best."

Today Molly Brant is honored as a founding mother of English Canada, and in 1986, a Canadian postal stamp was issued in her honor.

as 700 percent) and greed persisted throughout the war. Yet there were admirable exceptions. Thomas Paine, whose publication *The Crisis* continued to stir men and women to their highest goals, spoke out against profiting from inflation. He viewed the profit-makers with disdain, accusing them of "extinguishing by stages the ardor we began with, and surrendering by piece-meal the virtue that defended us."

Important support came from people like Haym Solomon, a Jewish immigrant from Poland in 1772 who had become a successful New York merchant by the time the war began. Captured and imprisoned twice during the war, he escaped each time. His primary contribution to the Revolution, however, was the donation of large sums of money to Washington at Valley Forge and the securing of loans and additional donations during the war. He died penniless in 1785 at age 45. There were other supporters, too, such as Christopher Ludwig, a German baker in Philadelphia, who promised to donate as many loaves of bread as he could make from flour provided by the Continental Congress.

As the war progressed, many colonial citizens faced hunger. A food shortage affected everyone, as troops from both armies scoured the countryside, taking whatever they could find. Continental officers seized what few stored supplies were found in villages along the way and often did not pay for them. Many transportation problems aggravated the supply problems. When supplies were finally located, often there

Haym Solomon provided financing that permitted the Continental army to continue its campaigns. *(National Archives, Still Pictures Branch, NWDNS-148-GW-1124)*

was no way to deliver them to the troops. It was not until the assertive Gen. Nathanael Greene was assigned by Washington as quartermaster in 1778 that such persistent problems were brought under control. By the 1780s, with the war dragging on much longer than they had anticipated, whole families temporarily left their homesteads to join their husbands and sons in the military camps. Washington despaired of moving whole regiments—plus camp followers—from place to place; he could not see how he would be able to feed them all. It was not long, however, before the staff of generals realized that without their families to provide some comfort and care for them, many of their men would simply leave for home. The food supplies were stretched thinner and thinner.

The final crushing burden of the war was the worthlessness of Continental currency. With the first announcement of independence, the Continental Congress established a money source for supplying the armies and paying wages. British currency soon became scarce, as casual contact and trade with the British ended. Continental paper money was created to take its place, exchangeable for silver or gold at the end of the war. This currency was never worth much, coming from a government and nation created out of thin air, or so it seemed. To add to the confusion, each state began to issue its own money, but this practice was ended by the Continental Congress in 1777.

At first, the supplies of paper money created an artificial prosperity, encouraging employment and allowing farmers to pay off their debts. However, from even the earliest days of the war, some farmers and merchants refused to take Continental money as payment, insisting on British coin. The currency problem increased each winter as self-serving suppliers throughout the colonies withheld items from the American army so they could be sold to the British, who had plenty of coin. As Washington wrote, people were "only restrained from supplying the Enemy with Horses and every kind of necessary, thro fear of punishm't." A British officer observed, "Notwithstanding they are displeased with our Government, they are not so with our guineas [coin]." Thus the British received large deliveries of supplies from the American countryside into the cities each winter, while the American soldiers suffered from great scarcity. Long after the Revolution ended, Americans would refer to things of no value as "not worth a Continental."

So in spite of the great victory at Saratoga and other encouraging military achievements in 1778 and 1779, there was little optimism in the Continental Congress, in the army camps, or throughout American villages and towns in 1779. In London, Lord North hoped the rebels would finally accept the hopelessness of their cause as financial ruin closed in. Even the most dedicated of American Patriots feared that the cause for independence was lost, and then surely all the Continental paper money in hand would be absolutely worthless. Inflation skyrocketed in 1780, and it soon took bushels of paper money to buy the simplest of wares.

Troop morale was extremely low. The winter of 1779–80 was one of "dreadful extremity" as it settled on Washington's troops at Morristown, New Jersey. The collapse of the value of American money meant even larger shortages than at Valley Forge. Food rations were cut to one-eighth for six weeks. Within four months, two major events occurred to reflect the distress of the colonial cause.

In May 1780, two of Washington's regiments from Connecticut took up arms in revolt to protest the intolerable conditions in camp and the lack of pay. The commander in chief was forced to use his Pennsylvania troops to put down the mutiny, but once order was reestablished, he fully pardoned all involved. (Seven months later, some 1,500 of the Pennsylvania troops at Morristown, New Jersey, would engage in their own mutiny—and there were several other such incidents throughout the war.) As their leader, Washington understood too well the extreme deprivation his men were suffering.

Then in September 1780, four months after the Connecticut mutiny in Washington's camp, came one of the most shocking and discouraging announcements of the war. Benedict Arnold, hero of Quebec, Ticonderoga, and Saratoga, was exposed as a traitor! Bold and brilliant Benedict Arnold had evidently seen the sad state of the American revolutionary effort, assumed that the British would soon be victorious, and could not resist the temptation to join the winners. But his motives went back longer and deeper than that. Arnold had long been rankled by the feeling that he had been passed over for promotions and that he had been unjustly accused of misdeeds during his service. After an injury at the Battle of Freeman's Farm outside Saratoga, he had to retire from combat duty, and in June 1778 he was assigned as military governor of Philadelphia. There he married a beautiful young Loyalist of that city's highest society. Soon he was having difficulty affording the expensive lifestyle he had come to enjoy, and he began to use his official position to improve his personal situation. Charged with various counts of abuse of his authority and financial impropriety, in January 1780 he managed to get off with not much more than a reprimand for two minor counts.

MONEY, MUTINY, AND MORALE

Benedict Arnold
(1741–1801)
(National Archives)

But by that time, he had already begun to provide important military information to the British army, and then he planned his major act of treason. He obtained command of the strategic post of West Point, above the Hudson River north of New York City, and he agreed to turn the fort over to the British for a large sum of money and other favors. In a dramatic turn of events, instructions for turning over West Point—in Arnold's handwriting—were captured from a British officer, Maj. John André, taken prisoner in late September 1780. The entire scheme was quickly exposed, but Arnold escaped into the safety of New York City and the protection of the British, who rewarded him with the promised sums of money and the rank of brigadier general. Like all traitors, he never was truly accepted by the other side, and he lived the final, restless 20 years of his life with no great success or respect.

The revelation that such an important member of the Continental army could have considered betraying the cause was just one more grim bit of news as the colonists entered the winter of 1780–81. There was no way anyone could have guessed that one year later, the great Yorktown campaign would bring victory to the exhausted and despairing American Patriots and launch them on the road toward a new nation.

11

"THE WORLD TURNED UPSIDE DOWN"

Prospects were grim for the war for independence in 1778. Washington's soldiers were briefly cheered by General Burgoyne's surrender at Saratoga, George Rogers Clark's victories in the western territories, and France's entry into the war. Yet the colonies were increasingly burdened by useless money, severe shortages of supplies, a critical and impatient population and a stalemated war.

In August 1778, after two years of military action in New Jersey and New York, Washington's army once again camped uneasily outside New York City. British commander Clinton's troops left the safety of New York Harbor only to terrorize the seaports of Massachusetts, Connecticut, New York, and New Jersey. Raiders on both sides made surprise attacks on outposts or coastal towns. In an amazing midnight attack guided by the black American spy Pompey Lamb, the daredevil "Mad Anthony" Wayne recaptured the Hudson River fort at Stony Point after one of the British raids had seized it.

Angered at continual British and Iroquois strikes against frontier settlements in upstate New York, Washington directed Gen. John Sullivan and Gen. James Clinton in the summer of 1779 to utterly destroy the Iroquois strength in New York. Nearly every Iroquois village and food source was burned in a systematic sweep from Albany toward Niagara Falls. The result, however, was not an end to Indian terrorism but an increase in raids of revenge carried out by the survivors, blazing on for years after the end of the American Revolution.

INVASION OF THE IROQUOIS HOMELANDS DURING
THE AMERICAN REVOLUTION, 1779

Lake Ontario

Ft. Oswego Mohawk R.   Ft. George

Ft. Brewerton
Oswego R.   Oneida   Ft. Stanwix
Onondaga Lake   Lake   Oriskany   Canajoharie
Canadasaga   Onondaga   GERMAN FLATS   Johnson Hall
Canandaigua   Ft. Dayton   Ft. Johnson
                Cayuga   Ft. Herkimer   Ft. Hunter
Genesee   Springfield
Canadaigua   Otsego Lake Cherry Valley Schenectady
Lake
Honeoye   Cooperstown   Cobleskill   Albany
Conesus   Schoharie
Kershong

Keuka   Seneca
Lake   Lake   Cayuga Lake   Onoquaga   Clinton
Catherine's Town

Newtown (Elmira)
Kanowaholla   Chemung   Unadilla

Battle of   Tioga   Ft. Sullivan
Newtown
Aug. 1779   Sullivan

                    WYOMING   VALLEY   Minisink
0   50 miles   Forty Fort
                        Wilkes-Barre
0   50 km
                Susquehanna R.   Delaware R.

▲ Indian villages   New York
● Non-Indian settlements   N
■ Forts   Easton
✳ Major battle   © 2000 Carl Waldman and Facts On File, Inc.

Scrappy assaults and counterattacks marked action at sea as well as
on land in 1779, and John Paul Jones's victory over the *Serapis* added to
a growing list of events that led Patriots to hope that the war was shifting in favor of the colonies. As battles flared, armies shifted, and ships
squared off, diplomatic maneuvers also played their part. In June of
1779, Spain joined France in declaring war on Britain. Soon thereafter
the Netherlands chose sides against England. Spain, however, did not
really favor independence for the colonies, because it feared future
American threats to Spanish colonies. Although Spain did not directly
aid the colonial effort in any major way, the Spanish fleet succeeded in
adding to the armed threat facing the British fleet.

In February 1780, the League of Armed Neutrality, led by Russia, brought eight other European nations into the conflict. The alliance tested British goals of maintaining a complete trade blockade against the American colonies, as well as the British Empire's reputation as ruler of the seas. In a determined mood, hoping for an end to the war, the Continental Congress worked for eight months in 1779 to arrange a list of peace terms for negotiator John Adams to present to the British Parliament in preparation for a peace treaty. Even though there was still no victory in sight, the congress forthrightly sought complete independence, boundary guarantees, and fishing and navigation rights from Great Britain.

Before 1778, the British strategy for victory focused on the northern cities as important seaports and centers of political power. Neither the British nor the Americans viewed the south as significant in winning the war. By February 1777, the Continentals had easily defeated the small Loyalist armies of the royal governors of Virginia and North Car-

A painting attributed to William Strickland, *Action between the Bon Homme Richard and* Serapis *off Flamborough Head, England, on 23 September, 1779 (National Archives/DOD, War & Conflict, #0048)*

olina, and no British regulars were placed in the south for combat. However, as the war dragged on and stalemated in the north, a new British plan emerged to shift the battleground to the south. Gen. Henry Clinton in New York urged that military campaigns be launched into the southern colonies. Backed by the British navy along the coast, these campaigns would open a new corridor to defeat the Continentals. Washington himself feared this very strategy.

While the British worked on a strategy for securing the southern colonies, the Continental Congress looked to the strength of the French fleet to break the stranglehold that the British warships had on the American seacoast. Great hopes were resting on the arrival of the French fleet in June 1778, under Admiral d'Estaing. French ships arrived too late, however, to ambush the British as they were evacuating Philadelphia. D'Estaing did not meet the British fleet, in fact, until July 10, 1778, many days after the successful British evacuation of Philadelphia. French ships again had an opportunity to defeat the British fleet in New York Harbor, but d'Estaing claimed his ships were too heavy to navigate the shallow entrance at Sandy Hook. As a result, neither side fired on the other. Washington then arranged a special American-French plan of action to dislodge the British from Newport, Rhode Island. When d'Estaing finally faced the British fleet in August at Newport, however, a sudden storm arrived to pound both navies, and the attack on Newport was abandoned.

D'Estaing was next called upon to support the American effort to recover Savannah, Georgia, which had fallen to the British in late 1778. True to British hopes, Georgia Loyalists had rallied at the recapture. By June 1779 the entire state was back in British hands and the royal governor back in office. Georgia Loyalists were proud to announce that they had "taken a Star and Stripe from the Rebel flag of America." Using the Savannah foothold, the British planned to begin their campaign up the coast to capture Charleston in the fall of 1779.

With the timely arrival of Polish count Pulaski's mounted troops in May 1779, American general Benjamin Lincoln managed to hang on to Charleston, resisting the first British attempt to gain the city. When the British retreated back to Savannah, the Americans pursued in hopes of recapturing that city. Admiral d'Estaing, with more than 33 ships, was called upon to lend his strength to the assault on Savannah in September. General Lincoln fired on the city by land, while d'Estaing bombarded it from the sea. Between the two of them, the French and

Count Casimir Pulaski (1748–1779). Copy of an engraving by
H. B. Hall *(National Archives/DOD, War & Conflict, #0061)*

Americans had more than twice the 3,200 British troops defending
Savannah. With cooperation and determination, it should not have been
difficult to seize Savannah and slam shut the back door necessary for the
British southern campaign to succeed. D'Estaing, however, refused to
wait for a long siege to have its effect on the British troops, and as a
result, General Lincoln found himself pressured into an early direct
attack on the city in October. The catastrophe left American forces bitter
about the great waste of lives—800 compared to the British dead of
155—and the hollow contribution of the French to the war effort. D'Estaing himself was wounded, and the valuable Count Pulaski was among
the dead. Veterans of the tragic attack compared it to the 1775 Battle of
Bunker Hill, in reverse. The smaller, protected British force had system-
atically slaughtered the waves of Americans sent under fire.

"THE WORLD TURNED UPSIDE DOWN"

D'Estaing withdrew his entire fleet in late October 1779, carrying more than 4,000 French troops, and returned to France, leaving the coast completely defenseless against the British fleet. It appeared that the longed-for French alliance was not going to rescue the crippled independence effort of the Americans after all. Events in the south went from bad to worse.

Charleston was the prize of the south, its economic and cultural center. After the British victory at Savannah in June 1779, Lord Cornwallis persuaded his superior, Sir Henry Clinton, to try an elaborate plan to seize the critical southern port and then move on toward New York. The American general Benjamin Lincoln had pulled back to Charleston with his militia forces, waiting for reinforcements, but the stout fort built of palmetto logs that had protected Charleston Harbor from British attack in 1776 was in very poor condition by this time. A powerful bombardment from Sir Henry Clinton's unchallenged English ships was matched by a sweep through South Carolina by British mounted and foot soldiers to the gates of Charleston. The city was forced into a desperate defense.

For a month, Charleston was surrounded and at the mercy of the enemy, its houses burning and its supplies cut off. Gen. Benjamin Lincoln's surrender of the city in May of 1780 was the most severe defeat suffered by the Americans during the entire war. More than 5,000 troops and three generals were taken prisoner, plus two fully

The siege of Charleston (British troops and artillery in foreground), May 1780 *(Library of Congress)*

Charleston

DOORWAY TO THE SOUTH

CHARLESTON, SOUTH CAROLINA, WAS A PRIMARY target during the American Revolution. As the largest city and the major seaport in the South, it was both a center of wealth and culture and also of the slave trade. Under the British system, North and South Carolina supplied England with many agricultural products such as rice, tobacco, cotton, and indigo. The southern colonies then purchased nearly all their manufactured goods from England, because they made few goods themselves.

Southerners resented the control of prices on both ends of the trade system. They were at the mercy of British prices set for their agricultural products, and they were stuck with British prices for goods they wanted to buy. When Bostonians began to protest the British taxes, southerners paid attention. When the port of Boston was closed by the British in 1774, the merchants of Charleston expressed their support and sympathy for the Bostonians. They shipped emergency supplies to other New England ports, where they were transported overland to Boston.

The British believed that if they could gain control of this doorway to the South, they could secure the southern colonies and move their armies north against Virginia. When hostilities broke out, the British attacked Charleston by sea and land in June 1776, but they were defeated at the Battle of Sullivan's Island. By late 1778, Savannah, Georgia, was under British control, and General Clinton counted on southern Loyalists to reinforce his ranks. In 1779, however, another British attempt to take Charleston failed. In the spring of 1780, Clinton placed the city under siege, and about a month later, the American forces there surrendered. Despite the seriousness of the loss of Charleston, it came too late for the British to use it as a doorway to victory.

equipped ships. At the surrender, a British officer observed that "the General limped out at the head of the most ragged rabble I ever beheld. . . . They laid down their arms. . . . The militia began to creep out of their holes the next day." The Continental Congress was devastated by the news, while Loyalists began to speak of "the beginning of the end." A jubilant Sir Henry Clinton sailed back to New York, leaving Lord Cornwallis to direct the defeat of the American forces in the south.

With the surrender of Charleston came also the news of a vicious massacre of mainly Virginian soldiers marching to aid the city during its siege. On May 19, at Waxhaus (or Waxhaws) Creek, South Carolina, some 350 of these men were attacked by British troops led by British lieutenant colonel Banastre Tarleton. The Americans tried to surrender, but Tarleton allowed his men to go on shooting or bayoneting until they had killed or wounded some 250 Patriots. After this, the war between the Patriots and Loyalists in the south became especially bitter.

During the deadly siege of Charleston, the Continental Congress ignored General Washington's advice and appointed their own favorite, Gen. Horatio Gates, to face Cornwallis in the South. Gates was given credit for the surrender of Burgoyne at Saratoga, although many questioned how much of that success was actually due to his leadership. The Continental Congress hoped that Gates would now rescue the South from disaster. When the Continental army reinforcement units arrived under Baron de Kalb, General Gates hoped to regain the American advantage in the South by taking Camden, South Carolina, in August 1780. It was one of the most savagely fought battles of the war. Gates's bad judgment led his confused troops into the bayonets of the British, and when his army lost heart, the general himself fled from the battle faster than his men, on his finest horse. General Gates's cowardice disgraced the entire cause for independence. Alexander Hamilton, later the first American secretary of the treasury, wrote: "Was there ever an instance of a general running away as Gates has done from his whole army?"

The Americans endured the loss of Baron de Kalb and more than 800 men, plus about 1,000 captured. Close on the heels of Charleston's surrender in May, the British victory at Camden in August was heartily hailed in London and saved Lord North's government from collapse. Once again, there were predictions that the rebels would soon beg for peace. Only John Wilkes and other Whigs in Parliament condemned the victory at Camden, saying it would actually prolong the war.

In September 1780, one month after the wretched collapse of Gates and the Continental army at Camden, there came to General Washington one of the bitterest messages of the war: Benedict Arnold was uncovered as a traitor. This added to the burden of the previous 12 months: Washington had lost the valuable Count Pulaski; he had

Bayonet charge by the Second Maryland Brigade at the Battle of
Camden, September 1780 *(Library of Congress)*

suffered the disastrous surrender of General Lincoln; he had endured
the disgraceful flight of General Gates at Camden; and he had faced
despair and near-mutiny among his troops wintered outside New York
City. It had been many years since the war had begun, and the struggle
for independence seemed almost hopeless to Washington and his
troops.

After four years of lost battles, cities, and countless men, however, the
prospects for American success suddenly and dramatically began to improve in 1780. Most of Europe was now lined up in opposition to Great
Britain, and Americans were relieved that at last the French had landed
troops to lend their help. The able French commander de Rochambeau
arrived at Newport, Rhode Island, in July with 5,000 French troops to
strengthen Washington's army, although they were quickly cut off from
the French navy by a British blockade of the harbor. Then, in the fall of
1780, the fighting in the south began to turn in favor of the Americans.

After defeating the rebellious colonials at the battle of Camden in
August 1780, General Cornwallis moved quickly through North Carolina, advancing toward Virginia with ease. As he fended off minor

militia attacks on his units, an important engagement occurred in October 1780 at King's Mountain, on the border between North and South Carolina. Frontier riflemen isolated a defiant Loyalist force on the mountaintop. Maj. Patrick "Bull Dog" Ferguson, the Loyalist commander, had boasted he would burn Patriot villages and hang their leaders. In spite of their weaker military position, the Patriot riflemen killed the brave Ferguson and forced the surrender of his unit. Much of the determination of the militiamen was in revenge for the terrible massacre at Waxhaus Creek, and it was only with great effort that their commander stopped them from killing all their prisoners in revenge. The Battle of King's Mountain on October 7, 1780, began the change of fortune for the Continentals in the South.

On the same day that the frontier Patriots won at King's Mountain, the Continental Congress finally agreed to Washington's request to appoint Gen. Nathanael Greene to replace the disgraced General Gates. General Greene arrived in Charlotte, North Carolina, in December 1780 with Baron von Steuben to train the troops as he had done at Valley Forge. He found the army "wretched beyond description," with barely 1,500 men able to fight. To complicate matters, the countryside was in rampant civil war, "the Whigs and Tories pursuing each other with little less than savage fury." Cornwallis's troops outnumbered Greene's, and the 38-year-old New Englander knew he would have to outwit Cornwallis if he was to have any success. Standard European warfare would never work under such circumstances, so Greene divided his small army in two for guerrilla warfare and to live off the land. Greene himself led one force, while the seasoned rifleman Daniel Morgan led the other.

The first test of Greene's strategy came on a frigid January morning in 1781 at Cowpens, South Carolina, near King's Mountain. With patience and efficiency, Morgan directed his troops so skillfully that they killed or captured almost 1,000 British, about 90 percent of the British troops engaged. In the thick of the cavalry charge was an African American, "too small to wield a sword," who saved the life of his commanding officer by killing a British officer with "a ball from his pistol."

Cornwallis lamented that the battle of Cowpens "almost broke my heart." Furious over the loss at Cowpens, Cornwallis pursued his victorious enemy, burning his own supplies and wagons because they slowed him down, as Morgan's troops rejoined Greene's. Greene led the British on a wild goose chase in and out of two states, humorously repeated in a merry ditty throughout the colonies:

Cornwallis led a country dance,
The like was never seen, sir,
Much retrograde and much advance,
And all with General Greene, sir.

General Greene finally chose a favorable site in sparsely settled western North Carolina near the brick Guilford Courthouse to face Cornwallis in battle. Washington had been able to send Greene reinforcements, and by March 1781, when he decided to take on the British again, Greene had more than twice as many troops as Cornwallis. He hoped his larger army would be able to overwhelm the British troops, which were now low on supplies and far inland, away from the crucial support of the British navy. In a "long, obstinate and bloody battle," many of Greene's troops fled from musket fire and the menace of English artillery—but they had forced Cornwallis to pay an enormous price. The British had more than 500 casualties—one-fourth of the British troops engaged—while American casualties were only about 300. Cornwallis's army had won the day but was desperately weakened. In London, it was said that another such victory would destroy the British army.

While Cornwallis pulled his troops back to the coast for food and supplies, Nathanael Greene spent the summer of 1781 working his way slowly from one British post after another in South Carolina until only the Charleston area remained securely in British hands. With him was an extraordinary band of men led by Francis Marion, all "distinguished by small black leather caps and the wretchedness of their attire; their number did not exceed twenty men and boys, some white, some black, and all mounted, but most of them miserably equipped." Under "Swamp Fox" Marion, this special unit managed to strike again and again at British forces much larger than theirs and then disappear into the swamps and woodlands. Stylish "Light-Horse Harry" Lee, father of Robert E. Lee, was sent by Greene to reinforce Marion's troops. In spite of their striking differences outwardly, Lee and Marion worked well together and combined their "light horse" forces (lightly armed cavalry) quite effectively.

While Greene's efforts whittled away at British strength in South Carolina, even his defeats were hollow victories for the British. With each encounter, the British lost more troops, often many more than the Americans. With the excellent leadership of men like Marion, Lee, and

Francis Marion, the "Swamp Fox," evades the enemy. *(Library of Congress)*

Daniel Morgan alongside him, General Greene developed an effective, hard-hitting and unconventional army. Taking only carefully calculated risks, Greene preserved his troop strength. Like Washington in earlier campaigns in New York and New Jersey, Greene was losing battles but saving his army and winning the overall campaign.

Just as General Greene was slowly wearing down British strength in the south, the colonies took their final steps toward an official, unified government. The Articles of Confederation had been ratified slowly, colony by colony, overcoming countless objections in various colonial assemblies since presentation of the Articles in 1777. With the final signature of Maryland in March 1781, the new form of government became law, and the Continental Congress became the "United States in Congress Assembled," the first time the United States was used as a proper noun. At about the same time, an office of finance was created to bring order to the monetary crisis tormenting civilian life and the war effort. As superintendent of finance, Robert Morris proceeded immediately to rescue the United States from financial chaos. He persuaded the Congress to authorize a national bank, institute a currency system based on coin instead of paper, and accept a new method of supplying the Continental army by contract. Monetary support and loans from France and the Netherlands gave the new system the boost it needed as it struggled to move the United States toward stability.

John Adams recorded so well the agonies of the Congress:

> When 50 or 60 Men have a Constitution to form for a great Empire, at the same Time that they have a Country of fifteen hundred Miles extent to fortify, Millions to arm and train, a Naval Power to begin, an extensive Commerce to regulate, numerous Tribes of Indians to negotiate with, a standing Army of Twenty seven Thousand Men to raise, pay, victual and officer, I really shall pity those 50 or 60 Men.

Meanwhile, General Clinton in New York was being hounded by Lord Cornwallis to bring his army to strengthen the remaining British troops in the south. Convinced that the war could be won in the colonies by attacking and securing Virginia, Cornwallis urged Clinton to support him. Clinton refused and, in doing so, left Cornwallis stranded, to pursue his objective alone. Like Burgoyne and William Gates in the 1777 British campaign to drive a wedge between New York and the New England colonies, the lack of cooperation between the two key British leaders in the 1781 southern campaign would lead eventually to catastrophe.

By May 1781, Lord Cornwallis had resupplied his troops and moved them to the small river port of Yorktown in Virginia, near Chesapeake Bay. While he was fortifying the town, a newly commissioned British officer arrived to add his troops to those of Cornwallis—Brig. Gen. Benedict Arnold. Arnold's forces had spent the past 16 months harassing Patriots in Virginia, including Governor Thomas Jefferson in Richmond. Thus, even without the support of General Clinton's New York forces, British troop strength at Yorktown numbered about 7,000. General von Steuben's American troops near Yorktown were greatly outnumbered until Washington sent Lafayette and Anthony Wayne's regiments to reinforce von Steuben.

French troops had waited for action since landing in Rhode Island in the summer of 1780. While Lord Cornwallis and General Greene moved back and forth throughout Virginia, Washington's Continental army, now backed by thousands of French soldiers, continued the watch outside New York City. British suspicion and fears increased that, with French support, the Americans would soon try to dislodge the redcoats

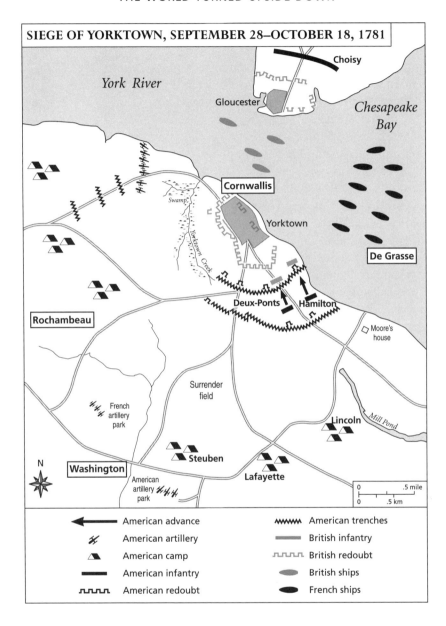

SIEGE OF YORKTOWN, SEPTEMBER 28–OCTOBER 18, 1781

from New York. Unlike Admiral d'Estaing, the French general de Rochambeau worked closely and cooperatively with General Washington, even turning over to him the command of the French troops and large sums of money from his own troops' support. In a clever and coordinated action in August 1781, Washington and General de Rochambeau managed to convince General Clinton that a major American attack on New York was coming. It is no wonder that Clinton refused to send troops to aid Cornwallis in Virginia.

In the summer of 1781, a special letter had been sent by Washington to Lafayette, laying out plans to attack New York City. When this letter fell into enemy hands, Washington decided to take advantage of this interception, shifting his original plans so as to appear in preparation for a major attack on New York City. In reality, he was secretly moving most of the Continental and French troops quickly to Virginia, adding to the combined forces of von Steuben, Lafayette, and Wayne. At the same time, a French West Indian fleet sailed for Yorktown.

French admiral de Grasse left the West Indies in August 1781 for Chesapeake Bay, reaching it in time to battle through the British naval blockade in September 1781 and drop anchor near Yorktown, cutting Cornwallis off from all British naval support. De Grasse's 3,000 French troops then landed to join the growing combined French and American armies surrounding Yorktown. By October 6, 1781, local Patriot militia had flocked to the American encampments around Yorktown, becom-

American forces besieging Yorktown capture strategic positions, October 14, 1781. (National Archives, Still Pictures Branch, NWDNS-148-GW-565)

"THE WORLD TURNED UPSIDE DOWN"

General Cornwallis surrenders at Yorktown, October 17, 1781.
(National Archives)

ing part of almost 20,000 allied troops facing Cornwallis's 9,750. The siege of Yorktown began.

Washington launched a heavy bombardment of Yorktown on October 9, 1781, moving quickly to bring Cornwallis to his knees. He knew that the French fleet would not stay in place past mid-October since de Grasse was under orders to return to the West Indies to protect the French islands. Washington had less than two weeks to seal the fate of the British at Yorktown.

The massive cannon bombardment destroyed most of the British earthworks in one day. For five days, there was, according to Dr. James Thacher, an army doctor present at the surrender, a "tremendous incessant firing from the American and French batteries . . . the [British] ships were wrapped in a torrent of fire . . ." On the night of October 16, the British attempted to escape the Yorktown entrapment by rowing across the Yorktown harbor to the British fortification at Gloucester, but Cornwallis's troops were forced by a sudden storm to turn back. General Clinton, meanwhile, had finally set out from New York with reinforcements for Cornwallis, but he was too late.

On the morning of October 17, 1781, a British drummer boy climbed atop a fortification to beat the drum of surrender. At 2 P.M. on October 19, French troops in crisp white uniforms marched into Yorktown with American troops in buckskins, homespun, and a scattered

General Cornwallis sues for peace before General Washington, October 19, 1781. *(Library of Congress)*

assortment of shabby uniforms. As the British and Loyalist troops laid down their arms, their bands played "The World Turned Upside Down." This popular folk tune of the period was the selection by the victors, a custom in surrender ceremonies. Receiving the sword of the surrendering British troops was Gen. Benjamin Lincoln, the man who had suffered the humiliating surrender of Charleston only one year before at the hands of Lord Cornwallis. Two more years would pass before a peace treaty would be signed to end the war, but the Battle of Yorktown was the last great battle of the War for Independence.

12
GLORIOUS TRIUMPH

As soon as the British surrendered at Yorktown, General Washington was eager to get the news to the Congress in session in Philadelphia. Congress, still responsible for financing the war, was hoping for any news that the end might be near. Washington sent Lt. Col. Tench Tilghman, a staff officer, to deliver the message. When Tilghman arrived in Philadelphia, it was early on the morning of October 22, three days after the surrender at Yorktown. An old watchman heard the news from the lieutenant and ran shouting through the streets. People began coming out of their homes, still dressed in their nightclothes, to celebrate the news, and Congress assembled at daybreak to thank God for the victory at Yorktown. It was hard to believe that only one year earlier the effort for independence had seemed so completely hopeless, with troop morale at its lowest and the colonial spirit exhausted by the war.

It was weeks before word of the outcome of the Battle of Yorktown reached England. When it did, both King George III and Prime Minister Lord North received the news in a state of frustration and dismay. The king felt angry and humiliated. He swore that he would relinquish his crown before giving in to the rebels. Lord North, shattered by the news, uttered, "Oh God! It is all over." He sensed that Cornwallis's defeat meant the end of the war for Great Britain.

Support for the war in Parliament had been declining for months. The struggle had been draining England's treasury for too long, and an increasing majority in the government argued that punishing the Americans any longer would be too expensive. The country had struggled through the French and Indian Wars just a few years before the

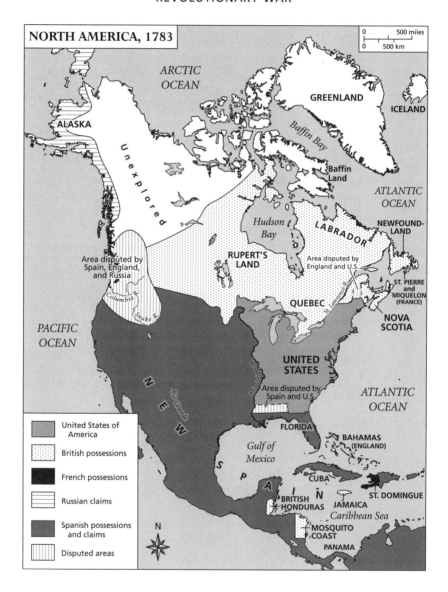

American Revolution began. The English were beginning to conclude
that money spent supporting an army 3,000 miles away was money that
could be spent on needs at home. News of Cornwallis's defeat at Yorktown persuaded even ordinary British subjects that perhaps it was time
to consider terms for a treaty.

GLORIOUS TRIUMPH

Although the decisive American victory at Yorktown was the last major battle of the Revolutionary War, the fighting did not end in October 1781. The British still occupied New York City, Charleston, South Carolina, and Savannah, Georgia. In fact, shortly after Cornwallis's surrender, Washington urged French admiral de Grasse to turn his guns on British fortifications at these three major cities on the Atlantic. De Grasse declined and followed orders from his government to take his fleet to the West Indies, where he would try to seize as much territory from the British as he could while also protecting French interests there.

As it turned out, there was no great, decisive battle after Yorktown to bring the war officially to an end. Washington's plans to force the British from Charleston and Savannah proved to be unnecessary. General Clinton lost his position as commander of all the British forces, left New York and returned to England. His delay in providing Cornwallis the support he needed at Yorktown caused his dismissal; when he arrived back home, he was regarded as a failure by his countrymen and eventually died in disgrace. Sir Guy Carleton replaced Clinton in May 1782, and shortly afterward he evacuated the British troops from Charleston and Savannah.

The only city still occupied by the British was New York. For two years after Yorktown, the Continental army remained in camp on the Hudson River outside New York and watched for any new movement by Carleton. Throughout the summer of 1782, messengers rode back and forth between New York City and the American encampments. The messages were secret, but there were rumors that the couriers carried with them the terms for a general surrender by the British. No one knew that peace talks had already begun. Benjamin Franklin was already in Paris and had begun negotiations with a British representative on April 12, 1782. It would be weeks, however, before news of a preliminary treaty would reach American troops.

There were some hostilities after the Battle of Yorktown, but they were scattered and had little impact on the war's conclusion. It was in Ohio that the final confrontations resulting in heavy casualties took place. In the frontier territories, the British had built a strong alliance with many of the Native American tribes. Combined forces of the Indians, Loyalists, and redcoats continued to attack frontier outposts in Kentucky, Pennsylvania, and the Virginia mountains. Among the casualties from these raids was Col. William Crawford, an old friend of Washington's and a business partner in land deals. Crawford was killed in an ambush at a frontier outpost at Sandusky, Ohio, in June 1782. Two months later, another American fort near Lexington, Kentucky, was overrun. The last Revolutionary War land battle took place on November 10, 1782, when George Rogers Clark led a force of more than 1,000 riflemen on horseback against the Shawnee. Clark and his band of wilderness sharpshooters burned the villages and defeated the Shawnee, who had terrorized the countryside, in a battle near Chillicothe, Ohio.

Although there was little fighting on land after Yorktown, the British fleet continued to attack American merchant and fishing boats up and down the Atlantic coast. New England privateers and fishing businesses were wrecked by ships of the Royal Navy sailing out of New York and Halifax, Nova Scotia. The French fleet was unable to protect American shipping, since de Grasse had sailed to the West Indies immediately after Yorktown.

De Grasse's decision to ignore Washington's appeal to remain in American waters turned out to be costly in the end. The French admiral did succeed in claiming one Caribbean island after another—until Sir George Rodney arrived to reinforce the British fleet stationed in those waters. Rodney and de Grasse met between the islands of Guadeloupe and Dominica in the battle of the Saints Passage, between April 9 and 12, 1782. The Royal Navy overwhelmed the French and even captured de Grasse.

De Grasse's defeat in the Caribbean took place on the same day that Franklin began talking with the British envoy in Paris, Richard Oswald, about a peace treaty. The effect of the surprising victory by Rodney was to give the British a stronger position in bargaining against the French in treaty negotiations in Paris. France felt that the help it had provided during the alliance—particularly its essential role in the victory at Yorktown—justified a claim to a major part in the peace proceedings. Even before the fighting ended on American soil, the French foreign minister, Count de Vergennes, addressed the U.S. Congress and persuaded it that American representatives sent to Paris for the formal treaty negotiations should not act without the approval of France.

Responsibility for representing the newly independent United States in Paris fell upon three men who had been influential in the Congress throughout the war: Benjamin Franklin, John Jay, and John Adams. Another American had been assigned as well, but Henry Laurens was a prisoner of war. As soon as treaty negotiations began, the British were forced to release Laurens.

John Adams
(1735–1826)
(Library of Congress)

Franklin was already in Paris, and he began the treaty talks on April 12, 1782. Probably no other American diplomat was more helpful to the American cause throughout the war than Benjamin Franklin. He was the one person most directly responsible for persuading the French to become allies of the American colonies. He also represented colonial interests in contacts with other European countries. Both Adams of Massachusetts and Jay of New York were well known and respected in America as members of the Continental Congress who had worked diligently toward independence throughout the long war. Adams had served as diplomat to France as early as 1778, while Jay had been sent to negotiate aid and support from Spain in 1779. A prosperous planter from South Carolina, Laurens served as president of the Continental Congress. He was captured by the British while on his way to Holland in 1780 to plead for loans for the Americans.

John Jay, the second member of the American commission to arrive in Paris, began work on June 12, 1782. Jay did not like the language of the preliminary draft of the treaty, which offered to deal with "the Thirteen Colonies . . . or any parts thereof." Jay insisted that the terms be directed to the Thirteen United States, a single sovereign nation.

John Jay (1745–1829) *(National Archives, Still Pictures Branch, NWDNS-148-GW-735a)*

Significantly, and perhaps unintentionally, if Jay had not demanded the revised language, there might not have been the need for the Americans to settle debts and other claims owed to the Loyalists and other British subjects who left the colonies during the war, since the first draft of the treaty did not mention a settlement of losses claimed by the Loyalists.

During the weeks while the language was being changed, news arrived of Rodney's defeat of the French fleet and his capture of de Grasse in the West Indies. As a result, Britain felt less vulnerable to the French in the negotiations. John Adams, the third principal member of the American treaty commission, arrived in Paris in October 1782, almost four months after Jay and Franklin had been negotiating. Adams had been in the Netherlands at work on a commercial agreement with the Dutch.

On September 27, 1782, Franklin, Jay, and Adams began formal treaty negotiations with Britain's commission headed by Oswald. In

November, after weeks of negotiating, the Americans decided to disregard instructions from Congress about waiting for help from the French in the negotiations. By November 30, the British and the Americans had worked out terms for a preliminary treaty. As it turned out, the terms of this preliminary treaty would remain unchanged and would be signed as the definitive treaty on September 3, 1783. According to the provisions of the treaty, France would gain no new territory in North America as a result of the war, although it still claimed most of the vast area west of the Mississippi River. The French did, however, win the island of Tobago in the West Indies and Senegal in West Africa. Spain received Florida in the treaty and still held much of the southwestern part of the continent as it had before the war. Great Britain lost all claim to the territory south of the St. Lawrence River and the Great Lakes in the eastern third of the country. The 49th parallel became the dividing line from the Great Lakes west to the Pacific. Such a separation would allow both countries to expand westward for years to come.

The Americans would have the right to fish in Canadian waters, as they had been doing for years, off the coast of Newfoundland and Nova Scotia. Any debts that citizens of either country owed the other side before the war would still be payable. Congress promised to advise individual states that they would be responsible for deciding what to do with property that belonged to Loyalists and British subjects. The last term of the treaty was to stop all fighting.

Britain agreed to terms in a treaty with France and in a separate treaty with Spain on January 20, 1783. All sides in the war then made arrangements to stop all fighting, an armistice was declared, and Britain announced an end to all hostilities on February 4, 1783. Afterward, Franklin tried to get Britain to agree to a commercial agreement with the United States. He even suggested that England, France, and the United States trade together peaceably. The French, however, were offended that the Americans had gone ahead and signed a preliminary treaty without their approval and showed no interest in helping the Americans get started as a new nation. The British, of course, were very resentful about the war and hoped the new country would fail.

Even though Britain declared an end to all hostilities in Paris on February 4, 1783, news of the armistice did not reach the United States until March 13. Congress declared an end to hostilities on April 11, 1783, a month after receiving the treaty from Paris. Two months later, on June 13, all but a few of General Washington's army began leaving the camp on the Hudson outside New York. Those who remained accompanied Washington and his staff into the city as soon as the British evacuated in November of that year.

Unfortunately for Washington, many of his soldiers were feeling cheated that they had not been paid for three months and would be going home with nothing in their pocketbooks. Officers, in particular, were angry over Congress's refusal to honor its promises to provide pensions and to pay what the country owed them for serving the last months of the war. They vowed to rebel against Congress's authority, but Washington persuaded them to be patient. Many of the officers had lost their fortunes, and some their homes, during the war. Some were faced with returning to their families with no income and no prospect that their lives would improve for years. Some of the men who served faithfully spent the rest of their lives in financial ruin. The only reward the private soldier received for loyal service was his weapon and a promise that he would be paid his last three months' wages eventually. The country's treasury was empty, and Congress could do nothing more than promise that once the country could afford it, the men would be paid.

The war meant financial ruin to many of the Loyalists as well. In April 1783, the last of them (about 7,000) left New York City. Altogether, approximately 100,000 British subjects had remained loyal to King George during the war; most of them fled at some point and went to Canada or back to Europe. After the peace settlement, Britain set up an agency to hear claims of losses made by the Loyalists. In truth, most of the claims were ignored by both the American and British governments.

After both sides had agreed to stop hostilities, there was only one more event that had to take place before the American people could feel fully independent from Great Britain. This event happened on November 25, 1783, when the last boatload of British troops left Manhattan and crossed to Staten Island before sailing for England. The British had occupied New York City since the battle of Long Island in the summer of 1776.

The same day in November that Carleton and the redcoats left New York, Washington and the few remaining men in his army reclaimed the city. Jubilant New Yorkers celebrated as the humble little army marched through streets that had not seen a Patriot soldier in seven years. The Americans did not have the breathtaking precision nor the spotless scarlet-and-white glamour of the British regulars. They stepped confidently and with authority, however, and they awakened among the

A New Nation in the World

THROUGHOUT THE AMERICAN REVOLUTION, THE American colonies reached out to other countries in Europe, especially France, for recognition and support. Once the war was over, diplomats from the new United States visited the courts and capitols of major nations to establish political connections and develop new trade agreements. The new American states could now also make independent decisions about social and economic issues such as slavery. Between 1776 and 1786, 11 of the 13 states either prohibited or heavily taxed the slave trade.

Throughout the Revolution, the colonies had to develop their own manufactured goods to replace English goods. In fact, the war not only halted trade with England, it disrupted trade among the American colonies. Each region pushed for more industrial development to meet its needs. Once the war ended, the homegrown businesses were up and running, ready to produce a surplus for international trade.

North American trade goods and natural resources were sought by many nations, and the economy of the newly independent nation flourished. U.S. ships sailed all over the world, flying a new flag: 13 red and white stripes with a circle of 13 stars on a field of deep blue in the upper left corner. Merchants were now free from British trade laws and the many restrictions that had funneled all goods and profits through English ports. Busy seaports such as Boston, Philadelphia, New York, and Charleston could charge their own import taxes on goods coming into the country, giving the fledgling states some income. Besides taxing foreign ships that arrived in their ports, they gave preference to goods arriving in American ships.

The newly formed nation was shaping its own course.

spectators a swelling sense of satisfaction, gratitude, and pride. They were the liberators.

Washington was accompanied by Governor George Clinton of New York to Fraunces Tavern on the evening of the same day he returned to the city. Owned and operated by "Black Sam" Fraunces, a West Indian, the tavern had first served as a favorite meeting place for Patriots early in the war. Once the British seized New York and British officers replaced Patriot leaders at supper, Sam Fraunces used his knowledge and discretion to aid prisoners of war and serve the cause

REVOLUTIONARY WAR

Washington bids his officers farewell at Fraunces Tavern, in New York City, December 4, 1883. *(National Archives, Still Pictures Branch, NWDNS-148-GW-179)*

of independence, later earning him cash grants and praise from a grateful Congress.

Clinton had arranged the occasion as an opportunity for the commander in chief to say farewell to his officers. Many of the men present were unable to hide their feelings, and tears rolled down their faces as they listened to Washington for the last time. The commander's hands shook and his voice cracked as he tried to control his feelings enough to speak to the men: "With a heart full of love and gratitude, I now take leave of you. I most devoutly wish that your later days may be as prosperous and happy as your former ones have been glorious and honorable." The men then rose to embrace the commander personally before he left the room and went out into the street to pass through a great crowd of New Yorkers who stood almost in reverence.

As a military strategist, Washington would not rank among the best in history, but as a leader who stayed in touch with his soldiers and influenced them to continue on in the most discouraging of times, George Washington was among the greatest. Even British officers admitted that a major reason the Americans won their independence was George Washington's leadership. He had every reason for losing the war: not enough men to fight, not enough weapons, not enough food or clothes, an unsympathetic congress. These are just some of the obvious disadvantages Washington faced every year of the war. He continued, however, because he believed that no one should be ruled by a tyrant.

During some dark times of the war, Thomas Paine had written inspiring words to encourage the Americans. *The American Crisis* was written in December 1776—just before Washington crossed the Delaware River:

> These are the times that try men's souls. The summer soldier and the sunshine patriot will, in this crisis, shrink from the service of their country; but he that stands now, deserves the love and thanks of men and women. Tyranny, like hell, is not easily conquered; yet we have this consolation with us, that the harder the conflict, the more glorious the triumph.

The Revolutionary War was indeed a hard and long conflict, the second longest war in American history. (Only the nine years of the Vietnam War were longer.) Eight exhausting years passed from the opening shot fired on Lexington Common on April 19, 1775, to April 11, 1783, the day Congress formally declared an end to hostilities. An estimated 233,000 men served during the eight years. Some volunteered for only a few months or even weeks of service and then returned home. There were never more than 38,000 men actively serving in the Continental army at any one time, and Great Britain did not have more than 40,000 serving against the colonials on any single date.

Because of the uncertainty about the exact number of men who served on the American side, the figures for casualties are not precise. One record lists total Americans killed in major battles at approximately 6,000, compared to 4,500 for the British; at least another 16,000 Americans probably died in prisons or of wounds received in battle. Sources vary widely on all such figures, but all agree that the American side lost more soldiers than the British because of bad food, food shortages, inadequate clothing, and generally bad conditions in camps. The winter at Valley Forge illustrates the effects of horrible conditions on the lives of the troops, when Washington commented that "you might have tracked the army . . . to Valley Forge by the blood of their feet."

America's Revolutionary War was in many ways unlike any other war in all of history, and it is still studied for the lessons it has to teach. Modern historians Henry Steele Commager and Richard B. Morris wrote this fitting summary to their book, *The Spirit of 'Seventy-Six:*

> The United States, born out of the travail of what John Adams called "this mighty Revolution," was the first colony to break away from a mother country and started a process whose end is not yet. It was the first of the new nations of the modern world, and for a long time a model to other new nations.

Even though Americans mark the Battle of Lexington and Concord as the beginning of the Revolutionary War, the struggle for independence really began years earlier. And this is not just an insight claimed by later historians. In a letter to Thomas Jefferson in 1815, John Adams wrote about the difference between the Revolutionary War and the spirit of independence which brought about the war:

> What do we mean by the Revolution? The war? That was no part of the Revolution. It was only an effect and consequence of it. The Revolution was in the minds of the people, and this was effected, from 1760 to 1775, in the course of fifteen years before a drop of blood was drawn at Lexington.

By the same token, it may be said that the American Revolution did not end with the ratification of a peace treaty on April 15, 1783. The truly significant revolution continued to at least the adoption of a constitution in 1787—and many would argue that the experiment of the American Revolution is still under way.

If the motivating force for the Revolution had to be summed up in a phrase, it would perhaps be "the search for individual liberty." This ideal has remained intact in America because it is based on a simple principle: Common citizens can exercise common sense and are able to govern themselves with reasonable and just laws. True, the United States is still a young nation when compared to many nations in the history of the world. There are critics who predict that government by the people, as practiced in America, will eventually fail, and that the United States

Thomas Jefferson (1743–1826) *(Library of Congress)*

will collapse just as have other great civilizations. In that sense, the disagreement between the Loyalist and the Patriot views of society still persists.

King George III of Great Britain and his supporters miscalculated the determination of the rebels in the American colonies. The United States may never have to fight another such oppressive foe, but each new generation of Americans must have the courage and will to stand up for individual liberty, just as the volunteers stood on Lexington Common on April 19, 1775.

Glossary

abstain   In a legislative or other official body, to choose not to vote on a measure.

armistice   A truce or agreement by warring parties to cease hostilities, at least temporarily but usually with the intention of negotiating a permanent peace.

blockade   To close a port, city, or region to maritime traffic and trade by the use of hostile ships or forces.

bound out   Contracted to work for someone for a specified length of time.

boycott   An organized effort to stop using or buying something as a means of protest.

brig   A small, two-masted ship, square-rigged on both masts.

broadside   In naval battles, to fire cannon directly at the side of an enemy ship.

Brown Bess   The colonists' nickname for the basic musket used by the British. The *brown* referred to the color of the wooden stock; *bess* is believed to be derived from *blunderbuss,* a name for an old fashioned firearm.

burgess   In colonial Virginia and Maryland, a member of the lower house of the legislature. The term is derived from the British word for a member of Parliament who represents a town or borough.

chandler   Originally referring to a maker and seller of candles, the word came to be applied to a merchant of special supplies; in particular, in ports it referred to suppliers of all kinds of gear and supplies needed by ships.

chattel slavery   Owning another human being as property; slavery.

coat of arms A shield bearing symbols and designs representing a family's heritage.

Continental money Paper money authorized by the Continental Congress during the American Revolution.

convoy Vehicles or ships traveling together for protection, usually with an armed escort.

courier An official messenger.

debtors' prison A prison for those who owed money; once a common form of punishment, they were abolished in most countries by the late 1800s.

draft A first or early version of a written work that will be edited and revised before it attains its final form.

earthworks Embankments or fortifications made from soil.

East Indies Islands and coastal lands of today's Malaysia and Indonesia; also called the Spice Islands.

emboss To impress paper with a raised design.

equestrian Related to horsemanship; an equestrian statue portrays an individual on a horse.

external taxes Taxes on goods bought from another country, such as tea, sugar, glass, and paper.

fife A small high pitched flute, often used to accompany drums in a military band.

flanking maneuver A movement around an opponent's side.

flintlock A gun that is fired by a small hammer striking on flint, which produces a spark to ignite the powder.

flotilla A naval unit smaller than a fleet but larger than a single squadron. It may also refer to a fleet of small ships.

foundry A place where metals are melted and poured into molds.

frigate A relatively swift, medium-size warship, with 28 to 44 guns on one gun deck.

grievance Complaint.

hardscrabble Poor quality, often rocky soil; it may also refer to attempts to make a living from working with such land or any kind of marginal subsistence.

GLOSSARY

Hessians   German soldiers from Hesse, a state in central Germany, hired to fight with British troops during the American Revolution. King George III's father and grandfather had been born in Hanover, the German state neighboring Hesse.

homespun   A plain, somewhat coarse woolen cloth woven at home on a loom.

howitzer   A cannon that shoots heavy shells over a long range and in a high arc that thus drops them on a target behind cover.

impressment   The kidnapping of men, often at sea but also on shore, to serve in the navy.

indentured servant   Someone who worked for another person for a specified amount of time under certain conditions, which were written into a contract, or indenture. Upon completion of the conditions, the individual was allowed total freedom.

inoculate   To introduce a small amount of a disease-causing material, such as a virus or serum, into a body in order to produce or boost immunity to a serious form of that disease.

internal taxes   Taxes on goods and services originating in the colonies.

Kentucky rifle   A long-barreled American firearm with a grooved, or rifled, bore that made it more powerful and accurate than a musket.

lobsterbacks   The American colonists' nickname for British soldiers, a reference to their uniforms' red coats that ended in split tails. See also **redcoats.**

Long Knives   By the mid-1700s, this was a nickname used by Indians, particularly those of the Great Lakes region, to refer to American colonial fighters. It referred to the colonists' use of long hunting knives and sabers. It has become most closely associated with the troop of Virginians led by George Rogers Clark in the Northwest Territory campaign during the Revolutionary War.

Loyalists   Colonial citizens who remained loyal to England during the American Revolution. See also **Tory.**

malthouse   A building for fermenting grain used to make alcohol.

maneuver   In the military, a strategic or tactical movement.

manslaughter   The unintentional killing of another person.

mercenaries   Soldiers hired to fight during a war.

midshipman   A person being trained to become an officer in the navy.

militia   Volunteer soldiers who are not part of a regular army but serve during emergencies.

minutemen   The American colonists' term for volunteer militiamen who were prepared to fight at a moment's notice.

Molly Pitcher   A nickname for any woman who aided Patriot troops during the Revolutionary War; it refers to the fact that these women often brought liquid refreshments to the fighting men.

mortar   A relatively small, portable cannon, loaded in the muzzle, that fires its shells at a low speed and short range but with a high, arching trajectory.

munitions   Any supplies related to weapons, such as gunpowder, ammunition, muskets, pistols, and cannons.

musket   A muzzle-loaded firearm with a smooth bore, good for short-range shooting. In colonial times it was fired with a flintlock.

mutiny   Open rebellion against military authority with the intention of seizing control of a ship or an army.

neutrality   A diplomatic position of not taking sides during a war.

palisade   A tall protective fence around a fort.

parliament   The chief legislative body of government, made of elected representatives. As a proper noun, it refers to the British legislature.

pound sterling (£)   The basic unit of measurement and value in British money.

portage   Transporting boats and goods overland between two bodies of water.

privateer   A privately owned and manned ship that has been commissioned by a government to attack and capture enemy ships.

Quaker   A member of the Society of Friends, one of whose beliefs was strong opposition to slavery. The term referred to an early leader of the group, an offshoot of Protestants, advising the followers to "tremble at the word of the Lord."

quarter   To house and feed someone; in the Revolutionary period, this referred specifically to Britain's insistence that the colonists house their troops.

ratify   To officially approve.

redcoat   A nickname for British soldiers, deriving from the color of their uniform's coat.

regular   In the Revolutionary War, a British soldier who belonged to the professional army.

repeal   To cancel a law or regulation.

revenue   In government, income usually raised by taxes.

royal governor   A colonial governor appointed by the king of England rather than elected by colonial citizens.

sexton   A person responsible for the care and upkeep of church property.

schooner   A coastal fishing and freight ship.

scrip   Colonial paper money issued during the American Revolution.

ship of the line   The largest warship of the navies of this period, usually carrying at least 64 guns. Its name refers to the fact that these powerful ships formed the first line as they sailed along in attacking enemy ships.

sloop   A single-masted ship supporting two sails, a mainsail and a jib.

squadron   A small group of ships that are part of a larger fleet.

staging point   A site for organizing and beginning a journey, project, or military operation.

sutler   A person who follows an army and sells it provisions.

Tory   In the American colonies, another name for those who remained loyal to the British king. It was borrowed from a British term for the conservative and royalist party and as the name originated from an Irish word for "outlaw," it was originally used in Britain as a term of contempt. See also **Whig.**

treason   The betrayal of one's country, especially by aiding the enemy.

Union Jack   The British flag, representing the union of England, Scotland, and Wales. A *jack* is a small flag flown by ships.

volley   A firing of many weapons or ammunition all at once.

voyageur   French for "traveler," in North American history it refers specifically to the people who traveled in remote areas to trade and transport goods for the fur companies.

West Indies   The Caribbean islands.

Whig   In Revolutionary times, a name sometimes used to refer to those colonists who supported the struggle for independence. It was borrowed from the name for one of the principal British political parties of that era; the word itself was based on an English word, *whiggamore,* that referred to Scots who opposed the British king in 1648.

writs of assistance   Unrestricted search warrants.

Further Reading

NONFICTION

Allison, Robert J., ed. *The Revolutionary Era, 1754–1781.* Detroit, Mich.: Gale Research, 1998.

Bakeless, John. *Turncoats, Traitors and Heroes.* Philadelphia: J. B. Lippincott Co., 1959.

Bliven, Bruce, Jr. *The American Revolution.* New York: Random House, 1996.

Bobrick, Benson. *Angel in the Whirlwind: The Triumph of the American Revolution.* New York: Simon & Schuster, 1997.

Bolton, Charles Knowles. *The Private Soldier under Washington.* Williamstown, Mass.: Corner House, 1976.

Bradley, Patricia. *Slavery, Propaganda, and the American Revolution.* Jackson: University Press of Mississippi, 1998.

Brandt, Clare. *The Man in the Mirror: A Life of Benedict Arnold.* New York: Random House, 1994.

Calloway, Colin G. *The American Revolution in Indian Country: Crisis and Diversity in Native American Communities.* New York: Cambridge University Press, 1995.

Carrington, Henry B. *Battles of the American Revolution, 1775–1781.* New York: Promontory Press, 1981.

Chidsey, Donald Barr. *The Loyalists.* New York: Crown, 1973.

Clarke, Clorinda. *The American Revolution, 1775–83: A British View.* New York: McGraw-Hill, 1967.

Clyne, Patricia Edwards. *Patriots in Petticoats.* New York: Dodd, Mead, 1976.

Cook, Fred J. *Dawn over Saratoga.* New York: Doubleday, 1973.

———. *Privateer of '76.* New York: Bobbs-Merrill Co., 1976.

Cullen, Joseph P. *The Concise Illustrated History of the American Revolution.* Yorktown, Va.: Eastern Acorn Press, 1981.

Daughters of the American Revolution. *African American and American Indian Patriots of the Revolutionary War.* Washington, D.C.: National Society of the Daughters of the American Revolution, 2001.

Diamant, Lincoln. *Chaining the Hudson: The Fight for the River in the American Revolution*. Secaucus, N.J.: Lyle Stuart, 1989.

Dolan, Edward F. *The American Revolution: How We Fought the War of Independence*. Brookfield, Conn.: Millbrook Press, 1995.

Ellis, Joseph J. *After the Revolution: Profiles of Early American Culture*. New York: Norton, 1979.

Fleming, Thomas. *The Battle of Yorktown*. New York: Harper & Row, 1968.

———. *1776: Year of Illusions*. New York: W. W. Norton & Co., 1975.

Greene, Jack P. *Understanding the American Revolution: Issues and Actors*. Charlottesville: University Press of Virginia, 1995.

Griswold, Wesley S. *The Night the Revolution Began, The Boston Tea Party, 1773*. Brattleboro, Vt.: Stephen Greene Press, 1972.

Hallahan, William H. *The Day the American Revolution Began: 19 April 1775*. New York: William Morrow, 2000.

Hansen, Harry. *The Boston Massacre*. New York: Hastings House, 1970.

Harper, Judith E. *African Americans and the Revolutionary War*. Chanhassen, Minn.: Child's World, 2001.

Hibbert, Christopher. *Redcoats & Rebels: The American Revolution through British Eyes*. New York: W. W. Norton, 1990.

Huey, Lois M., and Bonnie Pulis. *Molly Brant, A Legacy of Her Own*. Youngstown, N.Y.: Old Fort Niagara Association, 1997.

Ingraham, Leonard W. *An Album of the American Revolution*. New York: Franklin Watts, 1971.

Jaffe, Steven H. *Who Were the Founding Fathers? Two-hundred Years of Reinventing American History*. New York: Henry Holt, 1996.

Ketchum, Richard M. *Saratoga: Turning Point of the American Revolution*. New York: Henry Holt, 1997.

———. *The Revolution*. New York: American Heritage Publishing Co., 1958.

Knight, James E. *The Winter at Valley Forge: Survival and Victory*. Mahwah, N.J.: Troll Communications, 1999.

Lanier, Shannon, and Jane Feldman. *Jefferson's Children: The Story of One American Family*. New York: Random House, 2000.

Leder, Lawrence H. *America, 1603–1789. Prelude to a Nation*. Minneapolis, Minn.: Burgess Publishing Co., 1998.

Loescher, Burt Garfield. *Washington's Eyes: The Continental Light Dragoons*. Fort Collins, Colo.: Old Army Press, 1977.

Lukes, Bonnie L. *The American Revolution*. San Diego, Calif.: Lucent Books, 1996.

Marrin, Albert. *The War for Independence*. New York: Atheneum, 1988.

Mayer, S. L., ed. *Navies of the American Revolution*. Englewood Cliffs, N.J.: Prentice-Hall, 1975.

McCullough, David. *John Adams*. New York: Simon & Schuster, 2001.

FURTHER READING

McDowell, Bart. *The American Revolution: America's Fight for Freedom.* Washington, D.C.: National Geographic Society, 1967.

McGovern, Ann. *The Secret Soldier: The Story of Deborah Sampson.* New York: Scholastic Books, 1999.

Morpurgo, J. E. *Treason at West Point: The Arnold-Andre Conspiracy.* London: Mason/Charter Publishing, 1975.

Murphy, Jim. *A Young Patriot: The American Revolution as Experienced by One Boy.* New York: Clarion Books, 1995.

Nash, Gary. *Red, White and Black.* Englewood Cliffs, N.J.: Prentice-Hall, 1982.

Nordstrom, Judy. *Concord and Lexington.* New York: Dillon Press, 1993.

Perrin, N., ed. *The Adventures of Jonathan Corncob, Loyal American Refugee, Written by Himself.* Boston: D. R. Godine, 1976.

Quackenbush, Robert M. *Daughter of Liberty: A True Story of the American Revolution.* New York: Hyperion Books, 1999.

Randolph, Ryan P. *Paul Revere and the Minutemen of the American Revolution.* New York: Power Plus Books, 2001.

Sanderlin, George. *Journals of American Independence.* New York: Harper & Row, 1968.

Scheer, George F., ed. *Private Yankee Doodle, A Narrative of Some of the Adventures, Dangers and Sufferings of a Revolutionary Soldier, 1830.* Boston: Little, Brown, 1962.

Schultz, Pearle Henriksen. *Generous Strangers: Six Heroes of the American Revolution.* New York: Vanguard Press, 1975.

Smith, Barbara Clark. *After the Revolution: The Smithsonian History of Everyday Life in the 18th Century.* New York: Pantheon Books, 1985.

Stokesbury, James L. *A Short History of the American Revolution.* New York: William Morrow, 1991.

Szinanski, Leszek. *Casimir Pulaski: A Hero of the American Revolution.* New York: Hippocrene Books, 1994.

Taylor, Theodore. *Rebellion Town, Williamsburg, 1776.* New York: Thomas Y. Crowell Co., 1973.

Tucker, Glenn. *Mad Anthony Wayne and the New Nation.* Harrisburg, Penn.: Stackpole Books, 1973.

Walker, Bryce S., ed. *The American Story.* New York: Reader's Digest Association, 2000.

Ward, Harry M. *The American Revolution: Nationhood Achieved, 1763–1788.* New York: St. Martin's Press, 1995.

Wolf, Stephanie Grauman. *As Various as Their Land: The Everyday Lives of Eighteenth-Century Americans.* New York: HarperCollins, 1993.

Wright, Donald R. *African Americans in the Colonial Era: From African Origins through the American Revolution.* Wheeling, Ill.: Harlan Davidson, 2000.

Wunder, George. *Amateurs at Arms.* Harrisburg, Penn.: Stackpole Books, 1975.
Young, Robert. *The Real Patriots of the American Revolution.* Parsippany, N.J.: Dillon Press, 1997.
Zall, Paul M. *Becoming American: Young People in the American Revolution.* Hamden, Conn.: Linnet, 1993.
Zeinert, Karen. *Those Remarkable Women of the American Revolution.* Brookfield, Conn.: Millbrook Press, 1996.
Zell, Fran. *A Multicultural Portrait of the American Revolution.* Tarrytown, N.Y.: Benchmark Books, 1995.
Zobel, Hiller. *The Boston Massacre.* New York: Norton, 1996.

FICTION
Boutwell, Edna. *Daughter of Liberty.* Cleveland, Ohio: World Publishing Co., 1967.
Bristow, Gwen. *Celia Garth.* New York: Thomas Crowell, 1966.
Collier, James, and Christopher Collier. *My Brother Sam Is Dead.* New York: Four Winds Press, 1974.
———. *War Comes to Willy Freeman.* New York: Delacorte Press, 1983.
Cooper, James Fenimore. *The Spy.* New York: Penguin Books, 1997.
Edmonds, Walter. *Drums Along the Mohawk.* Boston: Little, Brown, 1964.
Fast, Howard. *April Morning.* New York: Bantam Pathfinder Editions, 1961.
———. *Seven Days in June.* Secaucus, N.J.: Carol Publishing, 1994.
Finlayson, Ann. *Rebecca's War.* New York: Dell, 1976.
Forbes, Esther. *Johnny Tremain.* New York: Dell, 1999.
Hopkins, Joseph. *Retreat and Recall.* New York: Scribner, 1966.
Kantor, MacKinlay. *Valley Forge.* New York: Lippincott, 1975.
Lancaster, Bruce. *The Big Knives.* Boston: Little, Brown, 1964.
Lawrence, Mildred. *Touchmark.* New York: Harcourt Brace Jovanovich, 1975.
Massie, Elizabeth. *1776: Son of Liberty.* New York: Tor, 2000.
Paretti, Sandra. *Drums of Winter.* New York: Lippincott, 1974.
Rinaldi, Ann. *Cast Two Shadows: The American Revolution in the South.* San Diego, Calif.: Harcourt Brace, 1998.
———. *The Fifth of March.* New York: Harcourt Brace, 1993.
———. *Finishing Becca: A Story about Peggy Shippen and Benedict Arnold.* New York: Harcourt Brace, 1994.
———. *The Secret of Sarah Revere.* New York: Harcourt Brace, 1995.
Taylor, David. *Storm the Last Rampart.* Philadelphia: Lippincott, 1960.

POETRY
Emerson, Ralph Waldo. *The Concord Hymn and Other Poems.* New York: Dover, 1996.
Longfellow, Henry Wadsworth. *Selected Poems.* New York: Gramercy, 2001.

WEBSITES

American History Archive Project. "American Revolution." Available online. URL: http://www.ilt.columbia.edu/k12/history/aha/arnav.html. Downloaded on April 2, 2002.

American Independence. Available online. URL: http://www.fordham.edu/halsall/mod/modsbook12.html. Downloaded on April 2, 2002.

The American Revolution. Available online. URL: http://revolution.h-net.msu.edu. Downloaded on April 2, 2002.

Thinkquest. "The Revolutionary War: A Journey Towards Freedom." Available online. URL: http://library.thinkquest.org/10966/index.html. Downloaded on April 2, 2002.

Index

Page numbers in *italics* indicate a photograph. Page numbers followed by *m* indicate maps. Page numbers followed by *g* indicate glossary entries. Page numbers in **boldface** indicate box features.

INDEX

183

INDEX

INDEX

INDEX

INDEX